THE CH... OF ROMULUS

A Short History of Rome

by G. B. Cobbold

Longman

The Children of Romulus: A Short History of Rome

Longman, 10 Bank Street, White Plains, NY 10606

Photo/text credits: Credits appear on page with photo.
Executive editor: Lyn McLean
Development editor: Barbara Thayer
Managing editor: Debra Watson
Text design adaptation: Vietnam by Murdoch/Crouse/O'Connell
Cover design: Elizabeth Prown
Cover photo: Bettman Archive
Text Maps: Elizabeth Prown

ISBN 0-8013-1371-6

1 2 3 4 5 6 7 8 9 10-DOC-99 98 97 96 95

UXORI FILIOQUE HOC OPUSCULUM DEDICAVI

I would like to thank the headmaster and trustees of Tabor Academy, who granted me the sabbatical leave during which the first draft of this book was written. I am also most grateful for the advice of my students and colleagues in the Tabor Classics Department, and especially for Dennis Herer's friendly and scholarly encouragement.

CONTENTS

PART I SPQR

Chapter One

THE FOUNDING FATHERS

ROME'S BEGINNINGS IN ASIA

*T*he story begins at Troy.

It is the tenth year of the Trojan War. Both the Greeks and the Trojans, the besiegers and the besieged, are exhausted. Even though the Trojans' best fighter, Hector, has recently been killed in single combat by the Greek champion Achilles, Troy still stands.

A blockade has not worked, nor has frontal assault. Only a trick, perhaps, can bring the city down. And so the clever deception of the wooden horse is devised by Odysseus. A huge hollow creature made of wood, its belly filled with armed Greek soldiers, is left conspicuously outside the walls of Troy, while the Greeks ostentatiously put out to sea. The Trojans are perplexed. Where have the Greeks gone? Why have they left behind the horse? What is the horse for? Is it some kind of offering to the Trojan gods? Some want to bring it inside the city, but Laocoön, Neptune's high priest in Troy, is highly suspicious. "I fear the Greeks," he says, "especially when they bring gifts."

However, at that very moment a pair of serpents come writhing out of the sea onto the beach, wind themselves around Laocoön, and crush him to death. Their message is clear. No one should listen to advice against welcoming the horse; anyone who gives such advice is doomed. Thus the horse, clanking occasionally, is dragged inside the city. The Trojans seize upon this event as an excuse to celebrate. By the

1

I.1 Greek vase-painting: Aeneas escaping from Troy with his father on his back, and with his wife Creusa following him. (Museum of Fine Arts, Boston)

small hours of the morning, after much singing and drinking and dancing, all the Trojans were asleep.

The Greek soldiers climb down from the belly of the horse. Through the darkness they flash a signal, and the Greek fleet silently rows back to the beach. Then the bolts on the city gates are drawn back and the Greek forces burst in.

The Trojans, still half-asleep and dazed, offer no resistance. Murder, looting, and arson ensue. The city is destroyed, its women and children are sold into slavery, and only a handful of the men escape. Among them is a certain Aeneas, who, with his father, his wife, his son and a few companions, makes his way through burning streets to seek safety in the nearby mountains. Although Aeneas's wife is lost during their flight, he is encouraged by his mother, the goddess Venus, to make his way westward and found a new city, at a spot under a grove of oaks where he will find a huge white sow with thirty piglets sucking at her udder.

Obediently Aeneas sets out. But on the way he has many adventures on the high seas and in foreign lands. He visits the Cyclopes in Sicily; he crosses the river Styx to the underworld, where he meets the ghosts of heroes of the past and the future; he is shipwrecked in Africa, and delayed there by the blandishments of Dido, Queen of Carthage (a city one day to be famous in Roman history). But the gods will not let Aeneas stay with her, and he departs for his final stopping place in western Italy, on the banks of the river Tiber, where he comes upon the white sow and her litter at last.

The region is called Latium, its people and its language Latin. The local chief welcomes Aeneas and promises him the hand of his daughter Lavinia in marriage. After a brief war with Lavinia's ex-fiancé, Aeneas marries her and founds a city, which he names Lavinium in her honor. Later his son Ascanius founds another city, Alba Longa, which thereafter is ruled for many generations by a dynasty of admirable kings.

ROMULUS AND REMUS

One day, there was a crisis in Alba Longa. King Numitor had been driven out of the city by his brother Amulius, and the king's daughter, Rhea Silvia, was locked up in order that she might produce no heirs to threaten the throne that Amulius had now usurped. Nevertheless, mysteriously and scandalously, she became pregnant by Mars, the god of war, and gave birth to twin sons, Romulus and Remus. Amulius then decided that the babies must be gotten rid of, yet their deaths must not seem to be his fault. He carefully placed them in a box, setting it afloat down the river, which was at that moment in flood. When the flood receded, the box was left high and dry and the twins were rescued by a wolf, who reared them until they were discovered by a neighboring farmer, who then brought them up in his house.

When the twins were grown, they joined a group of local teenagers where their qualities of leadership were so marked that it became clear that they were really of royal blood. Thus they were able to take charge of their group and lead it in rebellion against Alba Longa. They killed their wicked uncle and then restored Numitor to his throne. However, this first taste of power did not satisfy them. They resolved to establish their own city, which they founded at a bend in the Tiber on seven low-lying hills.

The construction of the new city was soon completed, except for the surrounding defensive walls. At this point an acrimonious discussion began between the brothers about which of them the new city should be named after. To settle their argument they sought the advice of the gods, which they believed would be revealed to them by the behavior of vultures flying high in the sky. But when the vultures eventually appeared, the brothers argued bitterly about how to interpret the meaning of their flight. In the end, Remus taunted Romulus by jumping over his half of the unfinished defensive wall. Romulus then lost his temper, picked up a rake, and killed his brother. So the city was called Rome, and this was the moment from which the Romans would calculate all subsequent dates in their history. In the modern system of recording historical events, the date was 753 B.C.

The city of Rome was filled at first by fugitives, refugees and outcasts—everyone who wanted to make a fresh start in life under a

I.2 Bronze statue: Romulus and Remus nursed by the wolf. The figure of the wolf is Etruscan, but the twins were added later. (Art Resource)

new regime. Romulus governed fairly with the advice of a group of a hundred older men, the fathers of the first hundred families he had accepted into his settlement. The group was called the Senate—or the *patres conscripti*—and from then on it functioned, with modifications, as the central institution of the Roman government. Under this system all went well until Romulus's sudden realization that there were too few women among his subjects—and women were essential to keep up the population. Therefore he decided to stage a festival to celebrate the anniversary of Rome's founding, and he invited the people of a nearby tribe, the Sabines, to attend. When everyone was absorbed in the celebration, Romulus gave a signal, and each Roman man seized a Sabine woman. The Sabine husbands were hustled away without a protest, and the population problem was soon solved.

That, at any rate, was the story. Although the Romans certainly enjoyed believing most of what they were told about Romulus, they did not accept all of it. For example, most Romans viewed the rape of the Sabine women as a myth. Nor was the tale of the twins' rescue by the wolf taken very seriously. It was probably invented to give Romulus the same kind of legendary respectability as figures like Oedipus, King of Thebes, and Cyrus the Great of Persia, who were also said to have been abandoned as infants and brought up by animals or shepherds. (At the other end of the Mediterranean, the Hebrews told a similar story about their heroic forebear Moses, who had been floated down the Nile and rescued from the bullrushes by an Egyptian princess.) Perhaps Romulus never existed—though a recently discovered inscription suggests that he did. It is clear, however—and supported by archaeological findings—that Rome began as a small village in Latium, and only very gradually became larger and more important than its neighbors.

Reading

Romulus Prophesies Rome's Future Glory (Livy: *History,* i. 16)

One day, when Romulus was inspecting the army on the Campus Martius . . . there was suddenly a violent thunderstorm and he was completely hidden from sight by a thick cloud; and from that time on he was never seen again.

The soldiers, who had been alarmed by the storm, recovered their nerve when the sun reappeared; but Romulus's throne was empty. The senators, who had been standing by him, said that he had been carried up by a whirlwind; the soldiers believed this story. Nevertheless they felt like children who had lost their father, and they stood for a long time in sad silence. Then some began to claim that Romulus had gone to heaven, and in the end everyone agreed that since he was the son of a god he was a god himself, and they prayed that he would forever be kind to them and protect them . . .

A man called Proculus later addressed the assembly, and he told the people that Romulus had left him the following message: "By the wish of the gods, my city will be the capital of the world. Let my people learn to fight. Let them be assured, and let their children be assured, that there is no earthly power that can ever resist the Romans."

LATINS AND ETRUSCANS

The inhabitants of early Italy were the descendants of Neolithic farmers. Their lives were difficult and demanding. They had to endure hardships of all kinds. They survived by displaying those characteristics that the Romans later always greatly valued in themselves— tenacity, seriousness of purpose, and the ability to put up with the worst in order to achieve the best.

However, the Latins of Latium were probably later arrivals, part of the major migrations into Italy that took place around 1000 B.C. Perhaps they were of the same stock as the Dorians, who at about the same time had made their way into Greece and occupied most of the Mycenaean citadels. The Latins settled in the west-central part of Italy, whenever possible in sites on hilltops, as a defense against enemies. The site of Rome—pigs and oak trees aside—was an especially advantageous one because it lay along a ford of the Tiber, and thus could control the north-south route which crossed the river as well as boat traffic up and down it. The Tiber was indeed one of the few navigable rivers in Italy, and because its mouth, at Ostia, was not regularly silted up, it could be used as a port.

At roughly the same time as the Latins were settling in Latium, another people were gathering just to the north, in Etruria (modern Tuscany). These people would later be called Etruscans. They may or may not have come originally from Asia, but there is no doubt that they grew very prosperous. The Etruscans were later to have a significant influence on the growth of Roman society. They were highly sophisticated and founded towns in which they developed an elaborate art and architecture. They sailed fast-moving ships and drove chariots. The Etruscans invented a system of writing for their language that used the Greek alphabet, and so can more or less be sounded out—although it has not yet been translated.

THE TARQUINS AND LUCRETIA

The story of Rome, according to the legends the Romans believed, continued happily after the disappearance of Romulus, who did not die but rather was snatched up into heaven (like the prophet Elijah). After him a sequence of seven kings—here the story is part legend and part history—ruled for two hundred and fifty years with varying degrees of benevolence. First came Titus Tatius, a Sabine who some say may have ruled jointly for a while with Romulus. After him came Numa Pompilius, a priest as well as a king, who organized Rome's religious calendar and oversaw a long period of peace. He was succeeded by the belligerent Tullus Hostilius, who first repulsed an attack from Alba Longa and then destroyed it. Tullus was followed by Ancius Martius, who spread Roman influence down the Tiber to Ostia. As a result perhaps of a subsequent alliance with the Etruscans or of Roman women marrying into the Etruscan royal family, the three last kings came from Etruria: Tarquinius Priscus, Servius Tullius, and Tarquinius Superbus (Tarquin the Proud).

There is archaeological evidence that the Romans early came under the cultural influence of the Etruscans, and were at least occasionally dominated by them politically, too. Much of the architecture of early Rome had Etruscan features—bridges, arches, and the main drain called the Cloaca Maxima (which still exists). The Romans also borrowed from Etruria the long, draped mantle called the *toga*, which Roman men always wore on formal occasions, as well as the *fasces*, or ceremonial bundles of sticks with an axe protruding from them. The fasces were carried by the *lictors*, the escorts of the Roman magistrates, and they represented the original power of the magistrates to inflict corporal or capital punishment. Many Etruscan gods, too, became the gods of Rome, and retained their Etruscan names even after they later became identified with the gods of Greece. The Romans also accepted the Etruscans' practice of seeking the will of the gods by augury—that is, by reading omens in thunder and lightning, in the behavior of birds, or in the arrangement of internal organs in sacrificed animals.

The last of the kings of Rome was the Etruscan Tarquinius Superbus. Unlike any of his predecessors, Tarquin was hated for his harsh edicts, his arbitrary cruelty, and in particular for the excesses of his son, Sextus Tarquinius. Sextus is supposed to have raped a woman called Lucretia, while her husband Collatinus was away at war. Lucretia, in mortification, stabbed herself to death, leaving Collatinus a vengeful widower. With three companions Collatinus swore an oath to expel the king. In 509 B.C., a bloody revolution broke out in the streets of the city, and Tarquin and his family fled to the Etruscan capital of Clusium.

The Romans then promised themselves that never again would they be ruled by a king, and in place of the monarchy a republic was established. Under the republic the city would be ruled by magistrates who were to be elected annually by all citizens—or rather, by all male citizens over the age of eighteen. The two chief administrative officers were called *consuls*. The first consuls were Collatinus himself and Lucius Junius Brutus, who ever after was popularly revered as the founder of the Roman republic.

Chapter Two

THE EARLY HISTORY OF ROME

ROME AND ITS PEOPLE

*L*ike many other city-states in the earliest stages of their development, Rome under its kings was a commercial center ringed by farming communities. Rome's inhabitants provided the goods and services that farmers had neither the skill nor the time to provide for themselves. Thus there gathered in the city all manner of craftsmen: manufacturers of wooden and metal tools, from ploughs to kitchen knives; clothing manufacturers and shoemakers; coopers and potters; wheelwrights, saddlers, and harness-makers; carpenters, stonemasons, and thatchers; and eventually, artists and musicians. Various middlemen for commercial transactions also flourished, including bankers, moneylenders, and shopkeepers.

All these activities, in the end, required supervision and organization. For this purpose, early village chiefs and shamans had evolved into kings and priests, or commonly combined both functions. As kings they made the laws for man; as priests they interpreted the will of the gods. They could threaten divine anger or exert their own authority to ensure obedience from the people; they could raise armies; they could make peace or war. When Rome became a republic, the powers of the priest-kings were divided between the new magistrates; even the chief priest—the *pontifex maximus*—was elected.

But the city was not only its citizens: It also became a physical conglomeration of houses, palaces, temples, law courts, workshops, and markets, all arranged about a central square, called in Latin the *forum*. The city then had to be linked to the farming countryside by roads and bridges, which were built by the people themselves or by the prisoners they captured in war and used as slaves.

ROMAN FAMILIES

The growing diversity of occupations inevitably divided the people into groups based on social class and wealth. But for all groups the basic unit of Roman society remained the family, and a Roman's names often were an abbreviated family history. Roman men and women had at least two names: a personal name (*praenomen*) and a family name (*nomen*). Sometimes a third name (*cognomen*) was added, which either described other family connections or some special achievement or physical characteristic of an ancestor. Examples of *cognomina* are Magnus (the Great), Naso (long-nosed), and Caesar (hairy).

The family consisted of everyone within a household, including slaves, ruled by the head of the family, the *paterfamilias*. In Roman law, he had the right to put to death his children and his slaves for any act of disobedience or disloyalty. He was responsible for the welfare of all his family members, especially the education of his children. For several centuries education took place entirely within the home (the first school was not established till about 200 B.C.), and at first the curriculum was very simple. In this period little Latin literature existed, and reading and writing were of limited use, even to the rich and powerful. But children certainly could be taught good behavior, particularly to defer to their elders and betters, to pay attention to the legends of heroes in the past, and to revere the gods—all according to the *mos maiorum*, or ancestral custom.

As important as ancestral custom were the ancestors themselves; not only were they seriously regarded as worthy examples of behavior, but they were also actually worshipped. Portrait busts of famous ancestors were prominently displayed, and their ashes were kept in a shrine within the house, along with the images of the household gods, the Lares and the Penates.

ROMAN SOCIETY

Roman families were divided into two groups, or social orders. One group was the aristocratic *patricians*, descendants of Romulus' first hundred senators, who had now become rich because they had early gained control of the best land. The other group was the *plebeians*, or *plebs*, who were the small farmers, the tradesmen, craftsmen, and unskilled workers. All patrician and plebeian men had the vote, but in other respects the two orders had separate social and political rights. For more than two centuries, the plebeians struggled to gain equality with the patricians.

The eventual fusing of the two orders so that all distinctions between them disappeared was a demonstration of the Romans' skill in changing their institutions without losing valued traditions. Roman society evolved unspectacularly like a bioorganism. In the first two hundred and fifty years of the republic's history there were few violent upheavals, and little drama. There were no famous reformers like Lycurgus in Sparta, or Solon or Cleisthenes in Athens. Though the Romans loved to argue and protest, changes in Roman life seem to have been part of an almost inevitable process, brought about as much by the patricians' realization that the time to share their power had come as by the unrelenting determination of the plebs.

The actual events in what is usually called the "Struggle of the Orders" were spread over many years and included a variety of social and political changes. The most sensational incident was the famous "secession," in 494 B.C. One afternoon the plebeians laid down their tools, walked out of Rome, and gathered peacefully on a hillside outside the city, where they listened to a speech by Menenius Agrippa. Their labor, he said, was as vital to effective government by the patricians as were the human stomach's digestive processes to the proper functioning of a person's arms and legs. And so he persuaded them to return peacefully to work. Some fifty years later, in 450 B.C., the Senate put up in the forum for everyone to see the so-called Twelve Tables—a list of the laws in force, which until then had never been published. These laws primarily involved contracts, inheritances, the emancipation of slaves, and the rights of women. From this time on, the Senate at least could not be accused of making arbitrary interpretation of the law to suit its own purpose. Then in 445 B.C. Gaius Canuleius (in the *lex Canuleia*) introduced an important amendment to the Twelve Tables that allowed patricians and plebeians to intermarry. The *lex Poetilia* of 326 B.C., which became necessary after a series of bad harvests, made it illegal to force anyone into slavery because of inability to pay off debts.

ROMAN MAGISTRATES

The government of the Roman republic succeeded in large part because the duties and responsibilities of its officials and institutions were clearly defined to serve the people's needs. They too, developed their functions during the struggle of the orders.

The *consuls,* first chosen in 509 B.C. on the occasion of the expulsion of the kings, were thereafter elected annually by the people. There were two of them, each with the right of veto over the other's action, in order that each might be properly checked and balanced. The consuls were the heads of state, invested by the Senate with *imperium*—the authority both to lead the armies of Rome in war and to oversee domestic and judicial affairs. The office originally was held only by patricians, but in 366 B.C. was opened to the plebs.

As the business of the state grew too complex for the consuls to manage alone, other magistrates called *praetors* were created to serve as understudies, to carry out the duties of the consuls during their absence from Rome in wartime. Eventually, however, the praetors' duties expanded, and their number increased to eight. The praetors were in charge of the lawcourts—one of them specialized in cases involving foreigners—and each year they published an edict announcing the legal principles according to which they intended to act. These edicts, collected, became the standard body of Roman legal precedent. Like that of the consuls, the office of praetor was opened to the plebs in 366 B.C.

The financial affairs of the state were in the charge of two (later six, later still, eight) *quaestors.* This was the first office for which the plebs became eligible, in 421 B.C.

Two *censors* did what their name suggests: they made certain that the citizen rolls were up to date, to make sure that no one could cheat in an election by voting more than once. The censors gained particular prestige, however, because they also had to keep up the list of the members of the Senate, and could strike the name of any member whose morality came into question. The censors also were in charge of public works in the city. The most famous censor was Appius Claudius (312 B.C.), who constructed both the first Roman aqueduct and the road named after him—the *Via Appia,* or Appian Way—that ran much of the north-south length of the peninsula and enabled the Romans eventually to extend their influence throughout Italy.

The *tribune of the plebs* was a special magistracy created after the secession of the plebs in 494 B.C. There were ten tribunes, who were elected solely by the plebs and committed to looking out for the interests of the plebs. Their persons, moreover, were sacrosanct; that is, it was illegal under pain of death to harm or even jostle them in any way (a forerunner of later immunity for diplomats). With the support of the majority of the people behind them, the tribunes of the plebs gained great power. They could propose legislation, and even more significantly, they could veto the act of any other magistrate, or even of the Senate itself, if they did not think that the plebeian cause was being served. And their devotion to their cause brought them often into conflict with the consuls and the Senate. On one occasion a senator named Coriolanus was so angry that free grain had been distributed by a tribune of the plebs during a famine that he raised a private army, and was only dissuaded from attacking the city by the frantic public pleading of his wife and his mother.

The *aediles* were originally the tribunes' assistants, little more than secretaries who kept records of the tribunes' business. Later they became magistrates elected by all the people, not just the plebs. The *aediles* were responsible for maintaining the accuracy of the weights and measures used in the markets, and for the cleanliness of streets and public buildings. Their job also included staging the games and gladiatorial shows that were often used to soothe popular discontent. Since the aedileship was an important early stage in a young man's political career, he would organize games which were as lavish and fantastic as possible, so that the people would later remember him with their votes.

All Roman magistrates were elected annually, and they served without pay. Thus only the rich could afford to stand for election. Since the city's wealth was largely in the hands of the patricians, this meant that, for the most part, only patricians were elected, even after all offices were legally open to plebeians. Furthermore, standing for office often became a family tradition. Those who could claim a consul in their family tree came to be called *nobiles* (nobles), and anyone running for consul for the first time in his family's history was looked down upon as a *novus homo* (new man). In fact, nearly 80 percent of the consuls elected between 234 B.C. and 134 B.C. came from the same twenty-six families, clearly demonstrating that this tradition also ran very deeply in the minds of the voters. The magistrates were in fact an aristocratic oligarchy with a common conservative point of view. Electoral contests were frequently less a matter of party politics and more a private squabble between two nobles.

THE SENATE AND PEOPLE OF ROME

The Roman *Senate* was the council founded by Romulus to advise the kings. During the republic the Senate remained in place to perform a similar function for the magistrates and for the people. Romulus' original hundred members grew to three hundred during the first years of the republic's existence, and was increased to six hundred about 80 B.C. Membership in the Senate was for life. Senators thus gained experience as well as great prestige, and were easily identified by the broad purple stripe they wore along the edge of their togas. To maintain their prestige and their aloofness from everyone else, they were not allowed to involve themselves in trade; nor could they leave Italy without the permission of their colleagues.

Vacancies in the Senate, originally filled by the king's nomination, were filled during the early republic by appointments of the con-

II.1 With their accustomed seriousness, Roman senators gather in their togas on the steps of a temple. (Art Resource)

suls or the censors. In 80 B.C., however, all ex-magistrates automatically became senators, which meant that eventually all members thus were indirectly elected by the people.

The advice the Senate gave to magistrates about domestic policy was greatly respected, and it was expected that the magistrates would take it. As a result, the Senate's opinions (*consulta*) virtually had the force of law. Though the Senate did not formally vote on the bills under discussion in the people's assemblies, it traditionally had the right to approve or disapprove them. This joint authority was signified by the letters SPQR (*Senatus Populusque Romanus*) that appeared in public places and on public documents. Only in matters of finance and foreign affairs (including the ratification of treaties) did the Senate have specific legal powers.

Depending on the topic to be dealt with, all the people—patricians and plebeians alike—would meet in one of two *popular assemblies,* one arranged by families, one by property classes. Yet for all practical purposes, they need not be distinguished. On the advice and under the guidance of the Senate, the Roman people, in these assemblies, made

laws, heard appeals against judicial decisions of the consuls and praetors, and declared war.

In 471 B.C., an assembly consisting of plebeians only, called the
concilium plebis (council of the plebs), was established. This assembly
elected plebeian tribunes and passed resolutions (*plebiscita*) that originally affected the plebeians alone. But the *lex Hortensia* in 287 B.C.
gave these *plebiscita* the force of law and made them binding on all the
people. The "democracy" of Rome was thus completed.

But Romans in reality were not particularly interested in day-to-
day politics, and as the number of citizens increased, and as more and
more of them lived farther and farther from Rome itself, fewer tended
to show up for meetings of the assemblies. As long as the people were
content, in fact, to leave the real decisions to the Senate, to allow the
Senatus consulta to make up much of the law and to elect the nobles
to office, Roman democracy (unlike that of fifth century B.C. Athens)
was more theoretical than real.

Chapter Three

THE GROWTH
OF ROMAN POWER

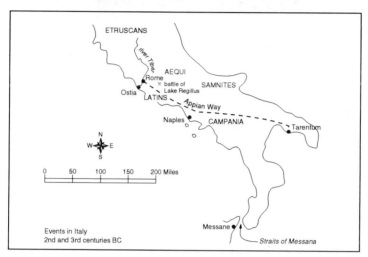

Events in Italy
2nd and 3rd centuries BC

*T*he passing of the *lex Hortensia* in 287 B.C. brought to an end the "Struggle of the Orders" that had shaped Rome's policies during its first two centuries. Meanwhile, equally important events were taking place outside Rome, as the comparatively insignificant city-state founded in 509 B.C. slowly gained control of all of Italy. Romans soon would discover that their evolving system of government was also able to serve them well during long years of military campaigns and diplomatic maneuvers.

ROME AND THE ETRUSCANS

After the expulsion of the kings in 509 B.C., Rome was invaded by the Etruscans, led by their king, Lars Porsenna, who was determined to restore the Tarquin family to the throne. However, the glorious Roman victories against the Etruscans are a blend of legend and historical fact that has only been partially documented.

From this Etruscan-Roman war came many of the famous legends about the gallantry and determination of their forebears that the Romans certainly hoped were true, but which, in any case, they proudly repeated to their children. They remembered how Horatius single-handedly held the last bridge across the Tiber against Lars Porsenna's army. They remembered how Quintus Mucius Scaevola (the left-

III.1 Portrait of an Etruscan and his wife, on the lid of their coffin. (Museum of Fine Arts, Boston)

handed), having set out to assassinate Lars Porsenna in his camp, stabbed the king's secretary by mistake; and how, when captured by the Etruscans, Mucius held his right hand over a naked flame, refusing to tell them Rome's military strategy and promising that all Roman soldiers could stand pain as well as he. They also remembered how Lars Porsenna, overcome with awe and apprehension, decided to release Mucius and to sue for peace.

Altogether the Romans waged war against the Etruscans for more than a hundred years. This period was one both of successes and setbacks. One particular struggle took place with the important Etruscan city of Veii. After a ten-year siege, Veii finally fell in 396 B.C. to a general with the resounding name of Marcus Furius Camillus, who was said to have driven a tunnel under its walls and to have emerged with his troops in the center of the city. In the end, Romans put down all Etruscan resistance, and absorbed the Etruscans into their territory.

III.2 Etruscan wall painting: a lyre-player. (Museum of Fine Arts, Boston)

ROME AND THE LATINS

At the same time they were at war with the Etruscans, the Romans were trying to take over the leadership of nearby Latin towns that had formed an alliance for mutual defense called the Latin League. As early as 496 B.C., the Romans fought a decisive battle with the Latins at Lake Regillus, where the twin gods Castor and Pollux were believed to have intervened on behalf of the Romans. The most interesting feature of the battle, however, was the first appointment by the Senate of a new kind of magistrate called the *dictator,* an official the Romans were to use in moments of crisis on many future occasions. The dictator had special *imperium* that overrode the authority of all other magistrates; but on the theory that if he could deal with the crisis at all, he could deal with it in six months, he was appointed only for a six-month period. It was considered that a longer term of supreme power would be dangerous to the system of checks and balances of power so carefully built into the Roman constitution.

Eventually, communication between the Latin cities was cut off by the operations of the Roman army, and the Latin League fell apart. In its place was established a confederacy of central Italian states, with Rome at its head. Each state was formally linked to Rome by a special treaty or alliance. Rome's treatment of its new partners seems to have been sensitive, and the Latin towns seem to have flourished under it. In future wars, most of Rome's allies here stood firm, and the Romans came to expect (and normally did receive) their loyalty. The test of this loyalty was not far off.

Reading

The Appointment of a Dictator (Livy: *History,* iii. 26)

[After a defeat by the Aequi, one of the tribes of central Italy] the city was in confusion, and the people were just as terrified as if Rome itself were under siege. . . . It was a moment for the Senate to appoint a dictator, and without objection Lucius Quinctius Cincinnatus was named. Now those people who think that money is all-important, and that only rich men can become powerful or successful, should look at the case of Cincinnatus: the only man who the Romans thought could save them was at this moment working on his small farm off to the west of the river. . . . The messengers from Rome found him hard at work preparing the ground for planting. "May the gods bless you and our country," they said. "Put on your toga, and listen to what the Senate commands."

Cincinnatus was taken aback; he asked if all were well, and told his wife to fetch his toga from the house. When it arrived, he wiped the mud off his face and put it on. The messengers then congratulated him on his appointment as dictator; they explained the military situation and required him to come to Rome. A ship, they said, was waiting to carry him down the Tiber. . . . In Rome he was welcomed by his sons, relatives, and friends, and by most of the senators assembled. Surrounded by this crowd, and escorted by lictors, he proceeded to his town house. The ordinary people who watched him pass were, however, less delighted: they were anxious about the dictator's power and how he might use it.

ROME AND THE GAULS

It was not only its neighbors in Latium and Etruria that Rome had to treat with and sometimes fight. By the end of the fifth century, Celtic tribes called Gauls, (frightening because of their shrill war-cries and their long wild hair) had wandered across the Alps and settled in northern Italy. In 390 B.C. the most restless and belligerent of the Gauls came swooping south, plundering their way through the territory of Rome's allies and finally threatening the city itself. A Roman army, greatly outnumbered, was severely defeated in a battle about ten miles north of Rome, on the banks of a tributary of the Tiber called the Allia. There now was nothing to stop the Gauls from entering and capturing Rome.

The memory of this humiliation was later blurred by a new crop of legends created to prop up Roman pride. As the Romans told the story, the Gauls entered the city like awestruck tourists, their eyes bulging at the magnificence of the streets and buildings. When they arrived at the Senate House and found the senators sitting silently in their official chairs, dignified and majestic as marble statues, one Gaul overcame his timidity and pulled a senatorial beard. The senator hit him, hard, with his walking stick—and with the tension thus broken the Gauls proceeded to ransack the city.

Only the central fortified hill, the Capitol, still held out, in the hands of a garrison led by Manlius. Its natural defenses, consisting of steep cliffs with no apparent handholds, had the Gauls baffled. However, they kept watch on the cliffs until they spotted a Roman soldier climbing down to fetch his helmet that had fallen over the wall. Watching carefully where he put his hands and feet, the Gauls worked out the route up the cliff to the fortress. Late that night, while the Roman garrison slept, the Gauls made their move. As they approached, the cackling of the sacred geese, who lived on the Capitol in the temple of Juno, raised the alarm. Manlius woke up just in time to order his men to the walls—and save the Capitol.

But the Capitol was besieged for several more months. The Gauls finally agreed to withdraw but only if they were paid a thousand pounds of gold. When the Romans protested that this was too much, the Gauls' leader remarked *"Vae victis"*—roughly translated as "Too bad." But his words reinforced what is always true, that in war the conquered should never have any expectation of justice from their conquerors. So the payment was made, and the Gauls did indeed depart—probably not, as the Romans later came to accept through their own legend, rolled back by the army of the famous Camillus, but more likely because of troubles at home in Gaul.

ROME AND THE ITALIANS

With the pressure from Gaul ended, and the city rebuilt, the Romans were able to renew their alliance with the Latin tribes. They then began to extend their power southward. They fought a series of wars against the Italian tribes to the south, particularly the Samnites, and subsequently founded colonies of Roman citizens throughout the region of Campania. Their progress was slow and unspectacular, but thorough. It was a time in which the Romans were able to polish the fighting skills of their army, with its phalanx-like legions of infantrymen, armed with short jabbing swords and javelins. And when the fighting was over, they made allies of those they had defeated.

Slowly the Senate began to think that one day the whole of Italy might be unified under the protection of Rome, and with this possibility in mind, it took its first step into building relations with other states. In 306 B.C., the Senate signed a treaty of nonaggression with Carthage, a prosperous city in North Africa that already possessed an impressive empire in the western Mediterranean. This treaty was intended to ensure that Carthage would make no hostile moves against Rome's allies along the west coast of Italy.

ROME AND THE GREEKS

The next Roman contact with another people was in the south of Italy, this time with the Greek towns that had been settled during the great wave of colonization from Greece in the eighth and seventh centuries B.C., when Rome was still ruled by kings. Southern Italy and Sicily had indeed become so dotted with Greek colonies that the region came to be known as Magna Graecia (Great Greece). But the Italian Greeks, like their counterparts on the Greek mainland, had always had difficulty in keeping peace among themselves. By 300 B.C., some of the colonists in Magna Graecia, seeing how effectively the Romans had dealt with the Samnites, requested Rome's help in their own local squabbles. The squabbles themselves were insignificant, but they became important when in 280 B.C. the city of Tarentum called on mainland Greece for support against what it considered as Roman interference.

King Pyrrhus of Epirus, one of the small fragments of Alexander the Great's old empire, was descended—or so he said—from Alexander himself, and he had similar ambitions. He therefore answered the appeal of Tarentum in the hope of achieving a quick conquest of the Greek towns of Italy, and then, perhaps, of persuading the members of Rome's Italian confederacy to join him in an alliance. Pyrrhus's army was well-disciplined and came complete with elephants imported from India—enormous monsters, that at first sight threw the Romans into a panic. In battle, however, the elephants were used only in the very first charge; after that they became so frightened by the smell of blood that they began to trample wildly about, and became equally dangerous to both sides.

Pyrrhus's incursion into Italy ended after a short campaign in which he failed to attain any of his objectives. He did win several pitched battles in 279 B.C., but his own losses were too great to tolerate, and none of the Italian allies moved to support his plan for an

MAJOR GREEK AND ROMAN GODS

Greek Name	Roman Name	Realm/Role
Zeus	Jupiter	King of the gods and mortals
Hera	Juno	Queen of the gods and mortals
Aphrodite	Venus	Love and beauty
Apollo	Apollo	Sun/prophecy/poetry
Ares	Mars	War
Artemis	Diana	Moon/hunting/childbirth/chastity
Asclepios	Aesculapius	Medicine
Athene	Minerva	Wisdom/arts, spinning and weaving
Demeter	Ceres	Fertility/agriculture
Hades	Pluto	King of underworld
Hephaistos	Vulcan	Fire/metalwork/thunderbolts
Hermes	Mercury	Messenger-god/trade/travel/thievery
Hestia	Vesta	Hearth and home/family life
Persephone	Proserpina	Ceres' daughter/cycle of seasons
Poseidon	Neptune	Sea and water/horses

III.3 The Appian Way, with original ancient Roman pavement, bounded by the ubiquitous Italian cypress trees. (Scala/Art Resource)

advance on Rome. In disgust and disappointment at his "Pyrrhic victories," he turned for home, and the Senate wasted no time in incorporating the Greeks of southern Italy into Rome's confederacy.

But this time the Romans gained far more than additional territory. They were particularly intrigued by this initial contact with Greek civilization, and religion was the first aspect of Roman culture affected. The Romans' traditional beliefs in leprechaun-like nature spirits had for generations been combined with the worship of Etruscan gods and Etruscan rituals. Now these Etruscan gods became identified with the more austere divinities of Mount Olympus, and they received their familiar Roman names.

THE ROMAN CONFEDERACY

By 279 B.C., the Roman confederacy included all of the Italian peninsula, and Rome had become so powerful in the western Mediterranean that the other states there were forced to take serious notice of it. The population of the city of Rome had grown nearly to a million inhabitants, of which perhaps three hundred thousand were men of military age. Another two million people inhabited the other towns and districts of the confederacy. The Roman army had just fought a war against a strong foreign enemy, a war in which Rome had received the willing support of a group of loyal allies—not only morally, but with fighting men. These allies paid no tribute, and military service was their only obligation to Rome; but it was a significant one, for they could produce enough soldiers nearly to double the strength of the legions.

Unlike the Athenian empire of Pericles the solidarity of the Roman confederacy was not maintained by force of arms. The confederate towns retained their own local governments, but were united by Roman law and order represented by visiting judges, by the spread of Latin as a common language, and by an evolving common culture. People and goods in the confederacy were transported along the "feathered arrows" of the Roman roads (so called because they always ran as straight as practicable and were lined with poplars and cypresses) and especially along the Appian Way, which had been completed in 312 B.C. Moreover, the inhabitants of an increasing number of towns near Rome were made full citizens or sometimes citizens with limited rights. The first tentative expansion of Roman citizenship, along with the creation of the system of alliances with other towns in Italy, took as long as the evolution of Rome's internal constitution, and it was achieved by the same determination and caution, applied particularly by the Senate. It was an imaginative act almost unprecedented in ancient or modern history to understand that temples, markets, water supplies, and drainage systems were much more effective than garrisons in keeping the peace within the confederacy, as well as in giving it strength to face its next great challenge from without.

Key Dates in Greek and Roman History (118–280 B.C.)

Dates (B.C.)	Events
1180 (traditional)	Fall of Troy—escape of Aeneas *travels of Odysseus*
776 (traditional)	*First Olympic Games*
753 (traditional)	Founding of Rome by Romulus and Remus
509	Expulsion of kings from Rome
506	*Constitution of Cleisthenes in Athens*
496	Battle of Lake Regillus against the Latins
490	*Battle of Marathon*
479	*End of Persian Wars*
471	Establishment of Council of the plebs
454	*Treasury of Delian League moved to Athens*
450	Publication of Twelve Tables
404	*End of Peloponnesian wars*
390	Gauls occupy Rome
323	*Death of Alexander the Great*
306	Rome's first treaty with Carthage
287	Lex Hortensia
280	King Pyrrhus in Italy

It is important to remember that the early history of Rome took place at the same time as much of Greek history. This chart shows some familiar events in Greek history and events that took place in Rome during these same years. (Greek dates and events are shown in italics.)

Chapter Four

THE FIRST PUNIC WAR, 264–241 B.C.

THE CARTHAGINIAN EMPIRE

Not long before Romulus founded Rome, according to the legend, a princess of Tyre, the Phoenician island-city off the coast of Lebanon, had fled to north Africa with a small band of followers. The princess's name was Dido. She was later identified with Queen Dido with whom Aeneas was said to have fallen in love, though the dates by no means fit. At any rate, she was supposed to have founded the city of Carthage.

By the beginning of the third century B.C., Carthage had become a large, prosperous power. It was ruled by a rich oligarchy supported by wealthy merchants and an army of well-paid mercenaries. The Carthaginians were highly competent seamen—a Carthaginian had sailed around the African continent while the Romans were learning to build bridges across the Tiber—who had established flourishing colonies in Spain and Sicily, as well as lucrative Atlantic trade routes that ran as far north as Britain and extended along the western coast of Africa. The Carthaginians had long shown an interest in spreading their influence into Italy, and at one time they had briefly allied themselves with the Etruscans. As early as 306 B.C., they signed a treaty with the Romans in which they promised not to encroach on the Italian mainland in return for assurances that Rome would not interfere with Carthage's colonies. However, a clash between the two seemed inevitable if Rome's expansion were to continue beyond the Italian mainland.

THE BACKGROUND OF THE CONFLICT

Given Rome's geographical location, it was not surprising that the first Roman expedition abroad would be to the island of Sicily. Sicily, with its flourishing Greek communities, lay only five miles away from the toe of Italy across the Strait of Messana. Equally clearly, the Carthaginians would undertake any military move against the Romans from Sicily. In 264 B.C. the citizens of Messana, the city nearest the strait and a colony of Carthage, rose in revolt and asked the Romans to support their rebellion.

The Senate debate on helping Messana was a long and anxious one. Without a fleet, the Romans were fearful of offending a great sea power. In any case, the Senate had no wish to break its treaty of 306 B.C. with Carthage. Some senators also feared that a war might weaken the traditional authority of the Senate, since war tended to stir political ambitions in the officers of obscure family who became popular with their troops. On the other hand, if a Carthaginian army overran the rebels in Messana and occupied their city, this would represent a clear, immediate threat to all the Greek towns of southern Italy. As part of the Italian confederacy, they looked to Rome for protection, and they were unwilling to tolerate the threat to their fellow-Greeks in Messana.

In the end, the danger that would be posed by Carthaginians so close to Italy convinced the Senators to take military action. Accordingly, a Roman army was ferried across the narrow strait and took control of Messana, which was at once blockaded by the Carthaginian fleet. War had begun—a war called by the Romans the Punic War, after the Latin word for Phoenician.

THE WAR BEGINS

Rome's first war-aim was to drive the Carthaginians out of Sicily. But to achieve this, an army alone, no matter how successful, would not be sufficient. The Romans also needed ships in order to control the sea-passage between Carthage and Sicily, as well as the strait of Messana.

There were few good natural harbors in the Italian peninsula. Moreover, the Romans had no warships and precious few transport vessels, certainly nothing that would stand up to the Carthaginian navy. As was usual for the Romans, however, necessity became the mother not of invention but rather of borrowing and of modification. They somehow got hold of a Carthaginian warship—their own story was that a Roman farmer stumbled across a wrecked Carthaginian vessel on an Italian beach and reported it to the Senate—and within two months they had made a hundred and twenty copies of it. (This feat of munitions manufacturing was to be rivaled only by the Soviet production of tanks and artillery in World War II.) Then, aware of their own inexperience in seamanship and particularly of their ignorance of naval warfare tactics, they developed a wide gangplank, which was kept lashed to the mast until a sea engagement began, when the plank could be lowered onto the deck of an enemy ship and hooked into place by an iron spike that resembled a bird's beak. From this spike the device was called the *corvus*, or crow. As a result, Roman infantrymen could cross the gangplank and engage the enemy on its own deck, exactly as they would on land.

The new Roman fleet, constructed almost miraculously, at once achieved equally miraculous success. The *corvus* worked well in its initial trials. Four quick naval victories gave the Romans command of the sea, so that they were able to land their legions in Africa for an attack on Carthage itself, and at the same time capture most of the towns of Sicily. But then things turned sour, and a long stalemate ensued. After much maneuvering, the Roman army in Africa was defeated, and its commander, Regulus, along with hundreds of his men, was captured. The Carthaginians released him on parole on condition that he return to Rome to arrange an exchange of prisoners, but he refused to recommend their proposal to the Senate. Instead, he returned to Carthage to be tortured, despite the Senate's plea to him to remain in Rome. But Regulus would not break his word, even to the enemy.

Meanwhile the Romans were also losing ships, some by storm and some in a battle that to the superstitious Romans was doomed to failure even before it began. When the Roman commander was informed that the sacred chickens had refused to eat that morning, he had them thrown overboard, declaring "Then let them drink." Despite their defeat, the Romans were able to rebuild their fleet—the Senate raised the funds by passing the hat amongst its members—at the same moment as the Carthaginians were laying up many of their ships to save money. The final battle of the war was fought off the Aegates Islands, after which the Carthaginians sued for peace. Carthage agreed to pay a huge fine to Rome and to evacuate Sicily. The Romans had achieved what they had set out to do, for Sicily now fell entirely under their control.

THE OUTCOME OF THE WAR

Sicily now became the first Roman province, or *provincia*, but it was not the only new overseas possession won by the Romans. After the war in 225 B.C. Sardinia and Corsica were captured from the Carthaginians, and they became the second province. At the same time, after more fighting with the Gauls, the area south of the Alps on either bank of the river Po, which was called Cisalpine Gaul (Gaul on this side of the Alps), became a Roman protectorate; and a new road, the Via Flaminia, was built to link it with the rest of Italy.

Three years later, the Romans again went to war, this time against the pirates of Illyria (roughly modern Albania and Bosnia) who had begun to attack Roman merchants now actively trading with the former Greek cities of southern Italy. As a result of their victory, the Romans now became interested in Greece itself. Rome opened diplomatic relations and began to trade with Athens and Corinth, who were also relieved to see the pirates' threat ended. Rome therefore established a protectorate in Illyria, to guard the sea route between Italy and Greece and to keep the region safe from King Philip V of Macedonia, who seemed to be interested in occupying it.

These Roman territorial gains were defensive; the Senate had no real desire to establish an empire. However, the Romans—whether they wanted to or not—had now become closely involved with the other Mediterranean powers. And they were not yet finished with Carthage.

Chapter Five

THE SECOND PUNIC WAR, 218–201 B.C.

OUTBREAK OF THE WAR, 218 B.C.

*T*he Carthaginian government wasted no time pining over the loss of Sicily. Instead, it immediately turned its attention to Spain, which for the moment was beyond the reach of Roman forces, and began to build up Carthage's strength there, under the command of Hamilcar Barca, the general defeated in Sicily. Hamilcar was driven by a deep hatred of the Romans, and by anger over their seizure of Sardinia. After the war ended, Hamilcar had made his son Hannibal swear an oath of revenge. In Spain Hamilcar's main objective was to raise a larger, a more efficient army to fight Rome again. He also founded the town of New Carthage (Cartagena) in Spain as a naval base. When uneasy Roman envoys asked about his intentions, Hamilcar swore with a straight face that his efforts were part of his plan to raise taxes in order to pay off Carthage's war debt. This excuse seems to have satisfied the Romans, at least for the moment. At any rate, in 226 B.C. Hamilcar signed a treaty with Rome in which he promised that he would make no move north of the Ebro River, while the Romans, in turn, promised not to move south of the river.

In 221 B.C., Hamilcar Barca died, and Hannibal, now twenty-six years old, succeeded him as commander in Spain. Remembering his oath, Hannibal then precipitated a crisis by besieging Saguntum, a town in Spain about a hundred miles south of the Ebro River in Carthage's sphere of influence, which was also an ally of Rome.

Was the treaty of 226 B.C. broken by Hannibal's action? Did Saguntum become allied with Rome after it had signed the treaty with Carthage? Was Saguntum excluded from the terms of the treaty because of its location? Whatever the truth of the matter, it is clear that Hannibal besieged the town in order to provoke war. As expected, the people of Saguntum appealed to Rome for help. However, the Romans were preoccupied with the Illyrian pirates, and for the moment there was little that they could do. But when Saguntum fell to Hannibal in the spring of 218 B.C., the Romans declared war on Carthage.

HANNIBAL INVADES ITALY

Hannibal sprang into action at once. He had the initial advantage over the Romans because he was able to mount an invasion of Italy from Spain with his best troops before the Romans could organize fully to meet him. For the longer term, however, the Romans had the advantage over Hannibal because they commanded the sea and had a greater depth of reserve forces at home. Nevertheless, Hannibal hoped that his lack of reserves would be offset if he could persuade Rome's allies to revolt and to join him when he invaded their territory.

Hannibal's first task was to cross the Pyrenees Mountains, which separated Spain from Gaul, and then the river Rhone. Both of these operations he brought off almost unopposed, though he had some difficulty ferrying his elephants (African ones this time) across the river. To do so, he had to construct a huge raft, cover it with earth and grass to make it look like a river bank, tempt his bull-elephants on to it by the lure of a cow-elephant in heat, and then tow the highly unstable load across the rivers. Despite his expectations, the local tribes resisted his forces, and the elephants' most useful contribution was to scare the tribesmen from making ambushes and guerrilla attacks.

Still ahead of Hannibal's forces were the Alps, daunting because of their reputation and terrifying in reality. The high Alpine passes were treacherous even in summer. There were precipices and landslides, and the snow melted unevenly, so that the Carthaginians would fall through an apparently solid surface into the freezing slush below. At the summit, Hannibal addressed his exhausted troops: by getting this far, he said, they had, in effect, climbed over not just the Alps, but the very walls of Rome. Victory now lay in the hollow of their hands.

The Carthaginian army was encouraged by Hannibal's words. Yet the descent was even more dangerous and difficult than the ascent because it was so much steeper and more slippery. At one point the path was completely blocked by a rockslide. Hannibal's men soaked the rocks with a makeshift acid—the soldiers' wine rations allowed to go sour—and then lighted bonfires to heat the rock, making it easier to split with pickaxes. Losses of men (perhaps a third of the total), horses, mules, and elephants were extremely heavy, and the army rested for four days in the sunny north Italian plain to regain its strength and recover its morale. The crossing of the Alps had occupied two weeks, and the main army's advance from New Carthage to Italy had taken nearly five months.

Clearly, the surviving soldiers soon completely recovered. Within days the Carthaginian army marched south, engaged the Romans in battle, and defeated them, mainly because of Hannibal's superior deployment of cavalry. Many of the Roman legionaries escaped, however, and a much more serious battle was fought the following spring (217 B.C.) on the shore of Lake Trasimene, about a hundred miles north of Rome in the Appennine mountains. Hannibal took up his position north of the lake on level ground, and waited there for the Roman consul Flaminius, who arrived late in the evening but in time to catch sight of Hannibal's army. Arrogant by nature, and criticized by his junior officers, who thought he was too impetuous, Flaminius determined to attack at dawn.

Even before it was fully light, Flaminius moved through the thick mist rising from the lake, marching his troops in column formation along the narrow path between the lake and the mountains. When he had advanced too far along the path to turn back, the Carthaginians attacked. Their light-armed infantry and cavalry had hidden in the mountains overnight. Now they charged down and caught the Roman force completely by surprise. For three hours the Romans tried to fight their way out of the trap, so desperately and so savagely that they did not even notice an earthquake that occurred during the battle. But they could not regroup effectively because they were unable to hear their commander's orders or see what they were doing in the mist. Flaminius then was murdered by his own disgruntled men. Fifteen thousand Romans were killed or drowned, weighed down by their armor. The rest straggled back to the city with news of their terrible defeat.

Although this was one of the worst defeats the Romans had ever suffered, the Senate did not panic. As it had before in moments of greatest crisis, the Senate again appointed a dictator, Quintus Fabius Maximus. After making sacrifices to appease what he thought must be the angry gods, Fabius developed a brand new strategy: The Romans must not allow themselves to be tempted into any more pitched battles, because they could not afford to lose more troops. Instead they would keep in constant contact with Hannibal, but avoid an actual clash, while they destroyed whatever food and equipment might fall into Hannibal's hands. To the Romans at home this strategy was unpopular; it seemed both craven and pointless. And indeed it was some time before it showed any success. But Fabius patiently kept on the move, often shifting his camp at night, always just out of the Carthaginians' reach but always within their view. That summer there were no more defeats. Hannibal was turned gradually southward, finding it harder to supply his troops as his lines of communication became longer. Now his men began to grumble, even to whisper of mutiny.

But by the next year (216 B.C.), Fabius's term of office as dictator had run out, and the consuls had grown tired of delay. They now looked for another opportunity to meet Hannibal in battle. They chose their spot on the coastal plain at Cannae, low on the calf of the Italian boot, putting their trust in their infantry, which still outnumbered Hannibal's, and discounting their weakness in cavalry.

At the beginning of the battle, the Romans broke through the Carthaginian line. However, the Carthaginian cavalry was waiting along each wing, and as the Romans advanced, Hannibal attacked on their flanks and in the rear. The Roman legions were again cut to pieces and put to flight. (Hannibal's successful "double encirclement" was to become a textbook maneuver, a tactic studied and copied in later centuries by other generals, including the American General Patton in the North African campaign of 1942.) The Roman defeat was complete. Rome and its allies lost fifty thousand men, including one of the consuls. Five thousand Romans were taken prisoner, and the rest scattered and fled into the countryside.

At this crucial moment Hannibal hesitated. Though urgently advised by his officers to mount an immediate attack on Rome, he decided to wait, and turned instead to plundering raids in the south. Hannibal evidently was waiting for some of the allied towns to come over to his side. However, only Capua defected, and he set up a permanent base there. His second-in-command reproached him: "You know how to win a victory, Hannibal, but not how to use it."

Hannibal's indecision may have been caused by the Romans' own unbending attitude. The Senate and the people did not despair, and the Roman allies in Latium remained loyal, blocking Hannibal's way to the city. The battle of Cannae had shown them, moreover, that Fabius' delaying tactics were, at least for the moment, the only successful way to hold Hannibal in check. Though the two sides might be roughly equal in infantry prowess, the Romans would not be able to defeat the Carthaginians until they had learned to overcome Hannibal's superiority in cavalry and could cut him off from his home base and reinforcements.

Reading

The Battle of Cannae (Livy: *History,* xxii. 51)

The next day at dawn, the Carthaginians came to collect the spoils and to look at the slaughter. Even they were appalled at what they had done. Thousands of Roman soldiers were dead;

infantry and cavalry lay together where the chances of battle had brought them, or where they had tried to escape.

In some places the Carthaginians found wounded men still alive, covered in blood and trying to struggle to their feet after they had been brought back to consciousness by the cold morning air. Some were quickly killed; others, with their legs nearly severed, begged to be finished off and stretched out their necks so that their throats could be cut. Still others had suffocated themselves by lying face downward in holes that they had dug in the mud. One soldier from Africa was found still alive, but most of his face was missing; he lay under a Roman who had died in the act of tearing at his enemy with his teeth.

CAMPAIGNS ABROAD

The Carthaginian government, aware that Hannibal's chances of capturing Rome itself were poor as long as the Italian allies stood firm, now hoped to encourage hostility to Rome from outside Italy, so that the Romans would find themselves encircled by foreign enemies. But Carthage would not or could not give its allies much effective support, and in the next phase of the war, Rome, by operating abroad, did better than it had at home.

First, Roman forces made successful raids by land and sea on the Carthaginians quartered in Spain, and many of the Spanish tribes came over to the Roman side. Though fighting continued for several years, the Roman grasp on Spain eventually tightened so much that Hannibal no longer could count on the overland route for supplies and reinforcements.

In 216 B.C. King Philip of Macedonia, hostile to Rome because of its occupation of Illyria, had made an alliance with Carthage. However, in skirmishes with Roman troops in northern Greece, Philip had received no assistance from Carthage and in the end was compelled to make a treaty with Rome.

Through the war, the towns of Sicily remained generally loyal to Rome, a mark of how efficiently Rome was governing this new province. In 214 B.C., however, the city of Syracuse had revolted against Rome after several months of internal confusion. The Romans sent a fleet and two legions (including some of the survivors of Cannae, who were given this opportunity to redeem themselves) to blockade Syracuse. But again, Syracuse received little help from Carthage. Yet the city held out for more than two years, thanks largely to the catapults and other gadgets designed by Archimedes, the famous philosopher—the same man who had run naked through the streets shouting "Eureka" after discovering in his bath the principle of displacement. In 212 B.C., Syracuse fell, and Archimedes, absorbed in a problem of geometry and thinking nothing of his danger, was killed by a Roman soldier. The southern bridge to Carthage was now in Roman hands more firmly than ever.

HANNIBAL'S LAST CAMPAIGN IN ITALY

Hannibal, meanwhile, was beginning to feel the pressure. Roman successes in Spain and Sicily were clearly affecting his nerve. Moreover, the Romans, despite their enormous losses of men in the battles in Italy, seemed to have inexhaustible reserves to replace them. Fabius was now consul; his delaying strategy had turned out to be popular, and his nickname, Cunctator (Delayer), which had at first been applied to him as an insult, now became a title of honor. Hannibal was kept penned up in the south, and Fabius was said to have saved the state.

At the same time as Roman forces were blockading Syracuse, others besieged Hannibal's Italian base at Capua. Hannibal tried to ease the pressure by marching on Rome, but his move did not draw off the besiegers. Outside Rome he learned that the Romans had raised yet another army, and he also heard the rumor—deliberately leaked to him by the Senate in a masterly stroke of psychological warfare—that the very land on which his army was encamped had just been put up for auction, and that the bidding was going through the roof.

In the face of such a display of Roman confidence, and perhaps remembering, too, how he had missed an earlier chance to take the city after the battle of Cannae, Hannibal turned away. He seems to have lacked the will even to return to take up the defense of Capua, which fell the following year (213 B.C.). It was, if not the beginning of the end, at least the end of the beginning.

ROME ON THE OFFENSIVE

Hannibal remained in Italy four more years. During this time he fought only minor skirmishes against the Romans, and Fabius, now reelected consul, captured Tarentum, another important town which had defected to the Carthaginians. In 207 B.C., Hannibal's brother Hasdrubal, in an attempt to bring him the reinforcements he so badly needed, broke out of Spain and made his way across the Alps with an army consisting mainly of Gallic mercenaries. But before he could join forces with Hannibal, Hasdrubal was caught between two Roman armies at the Metaurus River. At last the Romans were victorious in a major battle in Italy. By defeating this ambitious attempt to support

V.1 A Roman *eques,* or cavalryman. He goes into action somewhat unsteadily, for stirrups will not be invented until the Middle Ages. (Bettmann Archive)

Hannibal, the Romans not only effectively ended Hannibal's Italian campaign, but also turned the war in their own favor at last.

The victory at the Metaurus River was made doubly satisfactory by the news from Spain, where a brilliant young Roman general, Publius Cornelius Scipio, had isolated the last pockets of Carthaginian resistance and in 209 B.C. had captured New Carthage, Carthage's main base of supplies and stores. Scipio had learned the military lesson of Cannae: the Roman legions must become much more flexible in their movements and must combine their operations with the cavalry. By 206 B.C., Scipio was in complete control of Spain, which now became the third Roman province—and later was divided into Nearer and Further Spain.

At this point, Scipio wanted to take the war into Africa. Rome was now, almost by accident it seemed, the head of an impressive empire, but to retain its hold, it had to defeat Carthage decisively in its own territory. The Senate, however, was not sure whether to support Scipio; his plan was openly opposed by Quintus Fabius Maximus, whose caution with victory on the horizon was not as farsighted as his caution on the brink of defeat. Hannibal, he warned, was still in Italy, and no one could anticipate the dangers of a campaign in Africa or measure the Carthaginians' resistance when defending their own city. The job of Roman consuls and Roman armies was to defend Rome, not to go adventuring in foreign lands.

In the end, however, the Senate gave its approval to Scipio, who crossed over into Africa *via* Sicily, and at once set up a series of bases outside Carthage from which he might eventually attack the city itself. The Carthaginians now regarded Scipio with the same dread that the Romans had regarded Hannibal only a few years earlier. Hannibal was ordered to leave Italy and return to the defense of Carthage.

In the summer of 202 B.C., the two armies lined up against each other outside the village of Zama, near Carthage. However, Hannibal first asked for a conference to explore the possibility of an armistice. He and Scipio, two of the most distinguished generals in history, regarded each other with mutual admiration. Then Hannibal, without denying that he had been the aggressor from the beginning, and without expecting favorable terms, asked that the killing should stop. But Scipio was determined that Hannibal must be beaten, not forgiven, and the conference was a failure. Scipio became the first Roman general to face Hannibal in battle since the fighting at Cannae fourteen years before. At Zama, he was the only general ever to defeat him— ironically by his superior use of cavalry.

Hannibal escaped from the battlefield unhurt and persuaded the Carthaginian forces to surrender on what were reasonable, not revengeful, terms. Under the peace treaty, all Carthaginian ships and elephants were to be given up; in return the Romans would withdraw from Africa. Carthage would become a dependent ally of Rome, and would undertake no aggressive action against another state without the Senate's permission.

THE VICTORY OF THE ROMAN REPUBLIC

After the treaty with Carthage was signed in 201 B.C., Rome could sit back and congratulate itself on a remarkable achievement. It had retained its superiority at sea. It had won the defensive phase of the war in Italy because of good roads and the excellent fortifications of its towns, which had allowed Roman armies to move quickly and to rest safely. Moreover, the steadfastness and self-sacrifice of its allies had enabled Rome to wear down the enemy's will to continue the conflict. When they finally were able to take the offensive, Rome's citizen-soldiers, unlike Hannibal's mercenaries, had maintained their enthusiasm for their cause. And they had found in Scipio—nicknamed Africanus after the battle of Zama—a leader equally as brilliant and inge-

V.2A Detail of a relief carving of the port of Ostia: a ship is being readied for sea. Painted on the sail of the ship is a representation of Romulus and Remus. (Bettman Archive)

V.2B Detail of a relief carving of the port of Ostia. Neptune is overseeing the rigging of a ship. The elephants have perhaps been captured from Carthage. (Bettman Archive)

nious as Hannibal. Just as the Romans had won the first Punic War by modifying the Carthaginians' greatest advantage, the warship, in the Second Punic War Scipio had won decisively by adapting Hannibal's tactics and turning them against him at the battle of Zama.

But most of all it was a magnificent, grim demonstration of the best of the Roman character. The Senate and people, the crucial elements of the constitution, had not been deterred by disaster nor deflected by triumph. During many months of inactivity, they had not lost their patience nor their belief in a common cause. The republic had enjoyed its finest hour.

Chapter Six

CHALLENGES OF POWER

ROME'S FOREIGN POLICY, 201–146 B.C.

*R*ome had now become the strongest power in the Mediterranean region. Its relations with other states during the next fifty years would clearly demonstrate its dominance. In the East, Rome's might already had unnerved the rulers of the so-called Hellenistic kingdoms, the remaining segments of Alexander the Great's empire that were now ruled by descendants of his generals. The most powerful of these Hellenistic kingdoms were Macedonia, Syria, and Egypt, but they also included the confederacies and independent cities of Greece and the Greek states in Asia Minor.

Rome's earliest engagement in Eastern affairs had been its defensive campaign against the Illyrian pirates (217 B.C.). Then it had fought King Philip of Macedonia when he became an ally of Hannibal a year later. Now Rome entered into the complicated, obscure world of Greek politics, with the intention of eventually bringing the cities of Greece under Roman protection and control. Macedonia was finally broken up by 196 B.C. and became a Roman province ruled by a governor instructed to keep a watchful eye on the quarrelsome cities of Greece. In the end, however, Rome lost patience with the Greeks, and in 146 B.C. it sacked Corinth as a warning to the rest. Eventually, the Greek city-states, which had never united during the course of their history, would become a single entity, the Roman province of Achaia.

At the same time, Rome went to war with King Antiochus of Syria to end his interference with the Greek states of Asia Minor, whose freedom Rome had guaranteed. Hannibal, who had fled to Antiochus' court in disgrace after the Battle of Zama, encouraged his efforts, but Antiochus was defeated in 168 B.C. Nevertheless, his successor began to plan an invasion of Egypt. But he showed appropriate respect for the new Roman muscle when a Roman envoy drew a line in the sand and simply warned the Syrian ruler not to step across it. Egypt, Syria, and several of the states of Asia Minor thus became the first of the Roman "client kingdoms"—unofficial allies of Rome and defenders of Roman interests in the East.

THE THIRD PUNIC WAR, 149–146 B.C.

During these Eastern wars, Carthage had faithfully fulfilled its obligations as an ally of Rome and provided troops as they were required. However, Carthage broke its treaty with the Romans when it declared war on the neighboring state of Numidia, whose elderly but lively King Masinissa had for many years been conducting harassing raids into Carthaginian territory. Carthage finally struck back aggressively and, though its action was clearly provoked, violated its agreement with Rome. The matter might have been settled by negotiation but for the anti-Carthage faction in the Senate that was jealous of Carthage and still feared it. This faction was led by Marcus Cato, a conservative member who loudly denounced all foreign powers as potential enemies of Rome. For some time Cato had been in the habit of ending his speeches on any subject with the formula *"Carthago est delenda"* (Carthage must be destroyed).

Now Cato had found his excuse to urge the Romans into war, and the Senate, with some reluctance, responded by sending an army to besiege Carthage led by Scipio (the grandson of Scipio Africanus), who is said to have wept when he saw the splendor of the city he had been sent to conquer. When the Carthage fell in 146 B.C.—the same year as the sack of Corinth—its territory became the new province of Africa. By now Masinissa, who had started the trouble, had died, and Numidia, too, became a client kingdom of Rome.

The Senate was further persuaded to destroy Carthage entirely, to plough over the ground on which it stood, to pour salt into the furrows so that they could not be seeded, and to lay a curse on the site. The harsh punishment of the city can hardly have left a comfortable feeling in anyone's mind except Cato's. Though Carthage had technically broken the treaty, there was no reason to go to war with it again, and certainly none to wipe the city out. The incident did no credit to Rome nor to the spirit in which it had finished the second Punic War.

PROVINCIAL ADMINISTRATION AND POLICIES

The Roman system of governing its overseas provinces developed directly from its constitution. The Senate by decree extended the *imperium*, or the term of office, of consuls and praetors for up to three years. With this authority, these officials then were sent to a province to act as its governor, *pro consule* or *pro praetore* (in the place of a consul or a praetor), with the title of proconsul or propraetor. Quaestors and additional staff were added as required. The governorship of a province became a highly desirable opportunity for Romans, both to secure their financial future and to satisfy their political ambition. In fact, this frequently was the long-term objective of those who ran for office in Rome.

The most important and the most prestigious part of the governor's job was to command the military forces in his province, forces which were used to keep order there as well as to protect its borders. Rome's foreign wars were fought with armies led from the nearest province, so that the role of governor and commander became virtually synonymous. But a Roman governor also was the province's chief administrator and judge in its lawcourts. In addition, he was responsible for collecting taxes, and for constructing and maintaining public works such as roads and bridges.

In their daily administration, proconsuls and propraetors were not under direct control of the Senate. Nor were they subject to the veto of a tribune, as they would have been at home. In fact, the governors could behave in their provinces in ways they never would do in Rome, acting almost as a sort of king. Yet as Roman magistrates they were still unpaid. The temptation to use their position to plunder, extort, and embezzle must sometimes have been very strong. Indeed, by the middle of the second century B.C., there were many rumors of such wrongdoing, some doubtless true. At any rate, in 149 B.C. the Senate set up a special court (the *quaestio de rebus repetundis*) to prosecute governors who were accused of corruption.

However, this court always faced the possibility of a biased jury, because senators would be sitting in judgment on a member of their own class, and they themselves might have committed a similar offense, or might do so one day. A cynical joke circulated that a governor could make enough in his first year in office to pay off the bribes he had paid to get his job, that by the second year he could pay off the bribes for the court that would try him on his return, and that by the third year he could have made enough to live in comfort for the rest of his life. Yet the records of sensational trials of governors charged with wrongdoing do not support the joke. In fact, they were rare enough to show that the Roman sense of honor and honesty were still strong, and that the system must have worked well during these years. If nothing

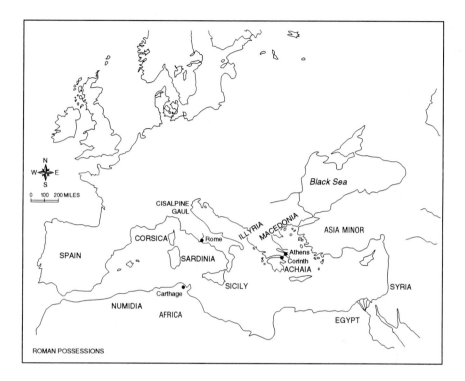

ROMAN POSSESSIONS

TERRITORY CONTROLLED BY THE ROMAN REPUBLIC, 146 B.C.

Provinces
Sicily
Sardinia and Corsica
Nearer and Further Spain (Hispania)
Macedonia
Africa

Protectorates (later provinces)
Illyria
Cisalpine Gaul
Greece (Achaia)

Client Kingdoms
Syria
Greek kingdoms in Asia Minor
Egypt
Numidia

else, the establishment of the Roman provinces and alliances brought comparative peace and unity to the whole Mediterranean and Middle Eastern region for nearly five hundred years.

The Romans did fight foreign wars in this period, but usually their conflicts were fought to protect or consolidate the borders of Roman provinces. There were few instances of Roman aggression or imperialism, certainly not in the second century B.C. But even the acquisition of its provinces, annexed as part of Rome's defensive strategy, made people like Cato anxious. The more provinces Rome had, he argued, the more magistrates it needed to govern them; the more magistrates it had, the less exclusive the Senate would be, and the more Rome's moral authority would be diluted and weakened.

Chapter Seven

NEW DIRECTIONS
FOR ROME

Rome's finest hour had ended with the Second Punic War. With their later involvement in the East and the establishment of new provinces, the Romans were never again as innocent, as morally high-minded. New elements came crowding onto Roman life, and though they may not have seemed important at the time, these developments soon would effect the direction of Roman society as a whole.

IMPERIUM

Cato perhaps had been wrong to provoke the destruction of Carthage, but he was not a fool. He was right to worry about the dangers of trying to use the institutions and practices originally developed for a small, homogeneous city to manage an empire that now extended throughout the Mediterranean. The increasing need to extend the *imperium* of magistrates, whether to govern provinces or to command armies on lengthy campaigns, had led the Senate to abandon an old rule that had prevented any official from being reelected until he had been out of office for ten years. During the Second Punic War, for instance, Quintus Fabius Maximus had been elected consul three years in a row, and Scipio Africanus had been either consul or proconsul for ten successive years.

By 195 B.C., the Senate had carefully worked out a set of rules called the *cursus honorum*: magistrates were to work their way up a ladder of successive offices, from quaestor to consul, with a minimum age fixed for holding each office. The Senate reasoned that to give a magistrate too much power, or to give it to him too soon, would encourage personal ambition rather than loyalty to the interests of the state. However, the Senate never succeeded in enforcing its rules regarding the *cursus honorum*, or for that matter any other checks on individual misuse of the *imperium*. It was one of the failures that, over the next hundred and fifty years, weakened and then led to the disintegration of the republic.

THE EQUITES

In the Roman army, the cavalry originally had been expected to provide their own horses, and to feed and stable them on campaigns. Horses were expensive, and their owners presumably had to be rich. As a result, the name *equites* (knights, horsemen) now became attached to a new class of prosperous men who were not in the Senate but had made money in business rather than from land.

The equites had first made their mark during the Second Punic War as members of private companies hired to transport supplies and equipment to Roman troops abroad. After the war they became involved in commercial ventures, in banking, in mining enterprises in Spain and Macedonia, and in foreign trade. They also collected—for a hefty fee—the rents from those who farmed the *ager publicus* (the land belonging to the state, which had been conquered many years before during the Latin and Etruscan wars). The equites were not as yet much involved in politics, and since they were not nobles, it would have been contrary to tradition for them to be elected to office. But they now were well off, even very well off, and they became extremely influential. Clearly, they would soon be ready to receive significant formal powers as well.

FAMILY LIFE

From 264 B.C. to 146 B.C. the Roman armies had been in action more or less constantly, especially since Hannibal's invasion, when the pace of recruiting had risen sharply. Many Roman men had been absent from home for five, ten, even fifteen years. Some had been conscripted at the time of their lives when they would normally have been thinking about marrying and setting up their own households. Others had just started families, which had then been forced to manage without them. During and after the wars, there was a steep increase in celibacy and in divorce. Many young men, young no longer, had become used to unmarried life and did not particularly want to change their status; many older men found that their wives had grown away from them and their children did not know them.

Of course, many thousands of Romans had been killed in action—more than sixty thousand in the battles of Lake Trasimene and Cannae alone—or who had died on campaigns abroad. Often a family's entire male line had been wiped out. Ever since the publication of the Twelve Tables in 450 B.C., Roman women had been allowed to possess property. Now many of them had inherited land or money, and were not only enjoying a comfortable life of independence, but were making important financial decisions and managing large estates. Women began to appear in public more frequently, at religious ceremonies and at the games. The daughters of noble families were often given the same education as sons, and in Rome groups of women gathered for intellectual and political discussions (like the Parisian salons in the late nineteenth century). But this new freedom for women did not afford them a more active political role, except as movers and shakers, behind the scenes.

SLAVES

As was true of most wars in the ancient world, Rome's conquests had resulted in large numbers of prisoners who were forced to become slaves. Though a body of law existed that was designed to look after the slaves' interests, Romans never questioned the institution of slavery itself. To them, as to the Greeks, slavery was an accepted, natural part of life. It did not become an issue for moral philosophers or social reformers until the arrival of Christianity, some two hundred years later.

Roman slaves fell into two categories: domestic slaves, and field hands who worked on the farms, especially on the large country estates called *latifundia*. The latter were very badly treated by any standard, because they were expendable and their labor was cheap. They were usually kept in chains, were miserably housed and fed, and worked under the whip. By contrast, private household slaves were by law counted as members of the family, and came under the authority of the *paterfamilias* just as did the children of the house. However, Roman families often became too dependent on their slaves. One of the most revered ideals of the Romans had been self-sufficiency; yet now they were waited on hand and foot by slaves, and they came to expect others to do everything for them. Thus, too many Romans became pampered and dependent.

Household slaves were paid a regular small wage (*peculium*) for their services, and many of them invested this money until they could buy their freedom. Alternatively, some were freed by their masters after long years of service. These freedmen (*liberti*) did not become Roman citizens themselves, although their children automatically became full citizens, with the right to vote. Perhaps the most distinguished Roman whose ancestors had been slaves was the poet Horace; there undoubtedly were many others, but presumably they were too embarrassed to admit to their background.

GREEK INFLUENCE

One of Horace's most famous lines succinctly describes the cultural effects of the Romans' exposure to the morals and manners of the Greeks. *Graecia capta ferum victorem cepit* (captive Greece took its crass conqueror captive), he wrote. Horace had seen the influence of Greece spread inexorably into every corner of Roman life, sometimes resented but generally welcomed. This Greek influence had begun with the absorption of the Greek cities of southern Italy after the war with Pyrrhus in 280 B.C. It had quickened during Rome's campaigns in Illyria and Macedonia during the Second Punic War, and became stronger still after Greece came under the protection of Rome in 146 B.C.

Politics
The Senate traditionally had been committed to preserving its own oligarchy, but also—more generously and wisely—to leading all social classes toward a common good. Rome was dedicatedly conservative, and it seldom welcomed changes in its policies, customs, or ideas. Now from Greece came the same kind of talk that had shaped Athenian politics, talk about the freedoms of individual citizens: the freedom to argue, to debate, to question the *status quo*. And soon the impregnable stone wall of the Senate, which had sheltered the Roman people through so many critical moments, would begin to crumble before the exploratory chipping of both altruistic and ambitious individuals.

In addition to Greek individualism came Alexander the Great's vision of the world as a pattern of infinite variety within a unity built upon a common set of values. This meant that the deliberations of legal theorists henceforth would have to consider both the concept of *ius civile* (law pertaining to Roman citizens) and *ius gentium* (law pertaining to humanity as a whole, as a part of nature). Even military strategy became tinged with Greek morality: in a modification of Aristotle's theory of a "just war" (a war in which Greeks must be free, barbarians must be enslaved) the mission of the Romans toward other states would soon become, in Vergil's phrase, *parcere subiectis, debellare superbos* (to be merciful to the downtrodden, but to crush the arrogant).

All this new thought, together with a loudly expressed enthusiasm for Greek art and literature, was introduced by an energetic group of young Roman nobles, led by the young Scipio and known as the Scipionic Circle. Conservatives, especially in the Senate—and especially Cato—regarded the Circle with suspicion, fear, and even hatred. Scipio and his friends, said the Senators, were soft themselves, and they were making other people lax too. In fact, they were undermining the whole fabric of traditional Roman seriousness and solidarity.

Private Life

A large number of the new household slaves were captives from Greece, and they brought their own Greek influences to the Roman families they served. For example, a slave who was sophisticated and literate might become a tutor to the children of the house. The introduction of Greek tutors led to a much wider knowledge of the Greek language, which became the mark of a liberal education, and Latin gradually became sprinkled with Greek words. Greek also was often used as the language of diplomacy (Hannibal and Scipio may have conferred in Greek before the battle of Zama), and it eventually became the *lingua franca* of the eastern part of the Roman empire.

But however good the slave was at his job, the distancing of the father from the education of his children meant yet another diminution of old-fashioned Roman conservatism, and opened yet another conduit for the new political and cultural ideas. A more luxurious style of life, which had become fashionable among the Greeks, now began to take hold in Roman homes influenced by their Greek slaves—and this further encouraged Romans' increasing self-indulgence. The Senate reacted by proposing new laws limiting expenditures on clothes, jewelry, carriages—and even on slaves themselves—but their measures had no effect.

Literature

The earliest examples of Latin literature consist of little more than songs, official inscriptions, long instructional treatises (Cato wrote one on agriculture) and clumsy comedies, and only fragments of them survive. Now the new familiarity with Greek culture brought a flood of Greek writing into Italy. Schools (*ludi*) had recently come into fashion for the children of the rich, and the poems of Homer became the core of the curriculum, just as they had been in Athens, along with Greek history, drama, and philosophy. These works not only were popular in themselves, but they served as models for a new generation of more sophisticated Latin authors. The study of Greek oratory by Roman lawyers and politicians, moreover, greatly influenced styles of public speaking and forensic argument.

Plautus and Terence wrote plays in Latin based on the "new comedy" of Menander. The latter usually were tales of ingenious slaves leading their masters through a trail of mistaken identities, new-found loves, and long-lost rich relatives. (The same plot later was copied many times: Shakespeare's *Comedy of Errors*, for instance, and the 1950s Broadway musical *The Boys from Syracuse* come from the same play of Plautus, and all P. G. Wodehouse's Jeeves stories follow the "new comedy" format.) There were also Latin versions of Greek epics, and, later, a long exposition in hexameters of Epicurus' philosophy by Lucretius called *De Rerum Natura* (The Nature of the Universe). Despite his majestic poetry, Lucretius' proposal that a mechanical arrangement of atoms was the basis of nature, together with his rejection of conventional religion, seemed to many to undermine the traditional Roman reverence for the gods—and thus was another blow at the *mos maiorum*.

VII.1 Country life: a farmer hands over a bull and a ram for sacrifice to one of the country gods. (Art Resource)

VII.2 A workshop in the city: craftsmen preparing lengths of material to be made into clothing. (Art Resource)

SOCIAL UNREST IN ITALY

When the Punic Wars ended, the family was only one Roman institution left weakened. The demobilized soldiers, returning home, often found that their farms had failed through lack of proper attention, or that their land had been sold and absorbed into someone else's estate. The *latifundia* thus had grown even larger at the expense of Rome's traditional small farms. Since it was much more economical to use slave labor, no jobs on the *latifundia* were available for citizens, nor was any land left for them to rent. These displaced and dispossessed farmers soon drifted into the cities, where they again found a glut of cheap labor. Eventually the unemployed began to outnumber the craftsmen and shopkeepers who originally had made up the urban population. They formed a large, restless underclass, distracted by lavish gladiatorial shows and chariot races, who lived off free or government-subsidized wheat—much of it imported from the new province of Africa. By these methods the magistrates and the Senate hoped to buy their patience and their votes.

Such entertainments and subsidies were not available, however, to Rome's Italian allies, who had fought so long and so well. They had won no profits from the wars and no perks; they had no vote in Rome which they might use to alleviate their plight. Silently and softly they began to press for a change in their status, for full Roman citizenship.

PART II The Roman Revolution

Chapter Eight

THE GRACCHI

TIBERIUS GRACCHUS, TRIBUNE, 133 B.C.

*T*iberius Sempronius Gracchus had impeccable connections. His father had been a distinguished governor of Spain and twice consul. His mother Cornelia was the daughter of Scipio Africanus, and after her husband's death she had received a proposal of marriage from King Ptolemy of Egypt. She was a famous intellectual, and had her children educated in philosophy by a Greek tutor. However, Tiberius Gracchus's political sympathies lay with the underprivileged. He had seen the misery in the countryside of Italy; he once remarked that Roman soldiers, after being exhorted so long to fight for the glories and traditions of their city, had in the end discovered that they had merely been defending the incomes of the rich. The conquerors of the world had no place to call their own.

In 133 B.C. Tiberius was elected tribune of the plebs, and he immediately introduced legislation to make more land available to veterans and other homeless citizens. There should be a limit, he proposed, to the amount of *ager publicus* (public land) which could be rented out by the state to any one man; the surplus land should be distributed in allotments. But many of the largest Roman estates consisted of land rented from the state for so many generations that it had come to be considered, to all intents and purposes, privately owned. Tiberius therefore further proposed that, as compensation, land re-

51

Events of the Roman Revolution, 133–31 B.C.

133	Tribunate of Tiberius Gracchus
123	Tribunate of Gaius Gracchus
107	Marius's war with Jugurtha
104	Marius's war with Cimbri and Teutones
100	Marius's Sixth Consulship; last tribunate of Saturninus
90	The Italian (Social) War
88	Sulla elected consul; war against Mithridates
83	Civil war: Sulla versus Marius; Sulla's dictatorship
79	Sulla's retirement
72	The Slaves' Revolt
66	Pompey's Eastern settlement
63	Cicero's consulship; conspiracy of Catiline
59	First Triumvirate; Caesar's departure for Gaul
49	The Civil War: Pompey versus Caesar
46	Dictatorship of Caesar
44	Assassination of Caesar
43	The Second Triumvirate
31	Battle of Actium

tained below the limit would be rent free for ever. The senators, of course, would be the group most affected by the new law. Since the measures were essentially reasonable, however, a majority of the Senate might well have accepted the measure as a personal sacrifice for the sake of the general good.

But Tiberius assumed that the Senate would be universally opposed. He therefore took his bill directly to the assembly of the people without consulting the Senate. This move was not illegal, but was without precedent in more than a century, and it was therefore certain to offend a Senate already anxious about its traditional prerogatives. The Senate struck back by persuading another tribune, Octavius, to veto the bill, as was his right. Tiberius immediately had the people vote to depose Octavius. Tiberius's measure was then passed, and the redistribution of the public land was organized by a specially appointed committee.

However, Tiberius was not finished, either with his reform program or with his challenges to the Senate. First, he announced his candidacy for a second successive tribunate—a move again not strictly illegal (because the tribunate was not subject to the rules of the *cursus honorum*), but certainly contrary to precedent. Moreover, it so happened that at this very moment the Roman client-king of Pergamum (in Asia Minor) had died and bequeathed to Rome all his assets, including his kingdom itself, which thus had just become the province of Asia. Tiberius therefore proposed that some of Pergamum's wealth should be made available to subsidize the newly settled farmers—a proposal that the Senate correctly viewed as interference with its role in both financial and foreign affairs, and thus none of Tiberius's business.

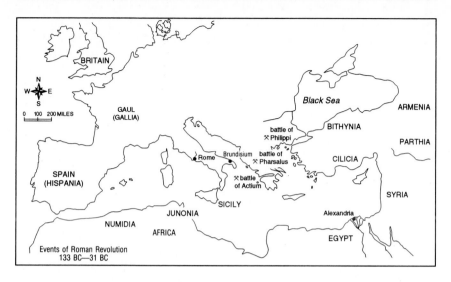

Events of Roman Revolution
133 BC—31 BC

The Senate could no longer contain its anger at Tiberius's affronts to tradition and to its own prerogatives. A group of Senators, armed with clubs, actually made their way into the meeting-place of the people's assembly. Both sides lost their tempers and then all control of the situation. In an appalling scene, unprecedented since the expulsion of the Tarquins many generations earlier, Tiberius and hundreds of his supporters were beaten to death and their bodies thrown into the river.

Reading

A *Tribune's Duty* (Plutarch: *Lives*, Tiberius Gracchus 15)

"A tribune of the people," argued Tiberius Gracchus, "is sacrosanct, and his person is inviolable, because the tribune's sacred duty is to guard and protect the people. But if he departs from this duty, if he oppresses the people or tries to tell them what to do, or prevents them from exercising their right to vote— then he should not expect to receive any honors or privileges, because he has not performed the duties in exchange for which the honors and privileges were granted him in the first place. Otherwise there is nothing to stop a tribune from making an attack on the Capitol or setting fire to a public building. A tribune who did such things would be a bad tribune; a tribune who fails to support the people is not a tribune at all. . . .

"A king—who holds complete power in his own person— holds a sacred office and is under the protection of the gods. But this did not prevent the citizens of Rome from deposing Tarquin when he did wrong. As a result of the crimes of that one man, the ancient monarchy of Rome was abolished. . . . A tribune cannot remain inviolate when he offends the people who gave him his inviolability; the people made him, and the people can undo him. The law makes it clear that he may take up his office if he is elected by a majority; should it not make it equally clear that he may be deposed by a majority?"

GAIUS GRACCHUS, TRIBUNE, 123 B.C.

Exactly ten years later, Tiberius's younger brother Gaius was elected tribune, in 123 B.C. and again in 122, this time without senatorial resistance. Gaius held ideals similar to his brother's. However, he was a more effective speaker—though he had a tendency to allow his voice to rise to a squeak and had to employ a slave to blow a low note on a pipe to remind him to calm down. Gaius also had carefully cultivated the habit (not unnoticed by Romans who were always on the alert for breaks with custom) of speaking in the assembly with his face turned not toward the Senate House, according to convention, but to the people themselves.

Gaius's proposals, all of which were passed without difficulty, again attempted to deal with the difficulties facing the rural and urban poor. The redistribution of public land was to be continued. The price of wheat in the city of Rome was to be fixed at a new low level. Colonies of citizens were to be founded in southern Italy and in north Africa near Carthage.

Gaius also set out to give some political power to the equites. His first suggestion, a good one, gave little offense to anyone, though the proposal, to enroll three hundred equites in the Senate, came to nothing. More provocatively, Gaius then had the assembly enact two laws involving the equites. First, the equites were to take over from the Senate control of the jury-courts, including the court which dealt with the cases of provincial governors charged with extortion. The equites also were to be given the right to collect the taxes in the new province of Asia. This last measure was intended to protect the Asians from greedy governors. But the transfer of authority over the courts did no more than set the Senate and the equites against each other. It in no way guaranteed fair verdicts, since the equites' decisions still might tend to be biased—but now would be anti-Senate rather than pro-Senate.

Again the senators were irritated, and they planned to get rid of Gaius before he could further damage their prestige. While he was absent supervising the establishment of the new colony in Africa, they spread rumors that its boundaries overlapped the site of the former city of Carthage that had been officially cursed in 146 B.C. Gaius, having been thus discredited, lost the election for his third tribunate. In a street scuffle soon after the election, a slave belonging to the consul Opimius was killed. This violence frightened the senate, which for the first time passed a special decree called the *consultum ultimum ut consules viderent ne res publica detrimentum caperet* (that the consuls see to it that the state come to no harm). This decree gave the Senate's moral support to whatever steps the consuls might find necessary to keep the peace, including the use of force. Gaius's remaining supporters became alarmed, and not knowing what to expect from the consuls, now rioted in earnest. Opimius had three thousand of Gaius's followers arrested and then executed. Gaius himself, despairing that the situation had slipped entirely out of his control, committed suicide.

Readings

Bad Omens Threaten Gaius's New Colony in Africa (Plutarch: *Lives*, Gaius Gracchus 11)

But in Africa, where Gaius was busy looking after the settlement of the colony which he called Junonia, near the site of Carthage, many dangerous omens were sent by the gods. A standard was wrenched from the hands of a standard-bearer by a gust of wind, and smashed. Another gust blew away the sacrifices which lay ready upon the altars, and spirited them off into the desert; and jackals carried away the freshly-planted boundary markers.

Memories of the Gracchi (Plutarch: *Lives*, Gaius Gracchus 18)

The Roman people, though hesitant and fearful at the time, soon showed publicly how they revered the memory of the Gracchi. They commissioned statues of the brothers and had them openly displayed; and the places where they had lost their lives were consecrated. The people would sacrifice there the first produce of every season's harvest. . . .

Their mother Cornelia is said to have borne her loss with calm nobility. She remarked that it was entirely apt that the places where her sons had died should be sanctified and that shrines should be set up there. . . . It was wonderful to hear her, later, talk about them without any tears or signs of mourning. Rather she would discuss their successes and their failures as if she were telling stories about the dead heroes of legend. Some people thought that old age or great grief had muddled her mind or hardened her heart, but they were themselves the ones devoid of feeling; they could not understand that a stern character and a strict upbringing will provide sufficient strength for anyone to overcome any sorrow.

THE LEGACY OF THE GRACCHI

Most of the legislation of the Gracchi met real needs and was effective, but their methods of having it passed had led to their own deaths—and to civic disaster. What had gone wrong?

If the Gracchi had wished merely to show that the Roman constitution was democratic in fact and not just in talk—that the decisions of the people did not depend on the approval of a senatorial oligarchy—they had amply succeeded. Yet the nature of the assembly of the people had changed since the influx of unemployed and unsophisticated former soldiers from the countryside. The assembly was no longer effective in promoting responsible democracy, particularly in matters requiring compromise or restraint. On the other hand, the brothers could have been accused of irresponsibility themselves. They had failed to consult the Senate at appropriate moments, they had overridden a tribune's veto, they had flirted with successive tribunates, and they had questioned the prerogatives of the Senate—each of these the action of demagogues.

If the Gracchi had deliberately wished to provoke the Senate, they had indeed succeeded. Yet the senators' savage reaction to this provocation was inexcusable. Just when the Senate needed to be firm and imaginative, it had descended to the level of the most unruly members of the city mob. Though the senators tried to regain their authority by impeaching Opimius for executing citizens without a trial, they spoiled the effect by instantly acquitting him—thus confirming the legality of the *senatus consultum ultimum* for future use. But above all, the Senate had shown that it was responsive to popular agitation, and the people had sensed its weakness. The effectiveness of violence had become clear to both sides.

Chapter Nine

MARIUS

*A*nother challenge to the Senate was not far off. During the next generation, irregular, even illegal, magistracies and commands ceased to be simply a matter of concern and instead began to pose a real threat to the stability of the Roman state. The first signs of crisis came in the career of an army officer, Gaius Marius. Marius had been elected tribune in 119 B.C., praetor in 114 B.C., and had then become governor of one of the Spanish provinces. Though he had been born a member of the equites, he had married into a noble family and seemed likely to become one of those exceptional men who would, as a *novus homo* (one who had no consul among his ancestors), become a consul. His big chance came in 107 B.C., and the occasion was the tiresome belligerence of an African prince called Jugurtha.

THE WAR WITH JUGURTHA, 107 B.C.

The trouble had begun five years earlier. In 112 B.C. Jugurtha had quarrelled with his brother over succession to the throne of Numidia, Rome's client-kingdom in Africa. This would probably not have been of any importance to Rome had not some Roman equites who were developing markets for business in Numidia been killed in the fighting. The angry citizens of Rome—especially the equites—immediately demanded a retaliatory attack.

Jugurtha was duly defeated and captured by Roman troops. He was then brought to Rome to give evidence at the trial of certain Roman officials accused of having accepted bribes from him. Then, when the trial was vetoed by a tribune in order to avoid a scandal over the affair, Jugurtha was alleged to have bribed the tribune. He left Rome with a famous parting crack: "Everything in Rome is for sale, if a buyer can be found."

The war in north Africa soon broke out again. Now the equites, anxious about their interests in Numidia, became even more impatient with Rome's slow progress in the conflict. Under pressure from the equites, the people decided that Marius, who had gained a solid military reputation in Spain, was the man for the job. In 107 B.C. they elected him consul with the special proviso that he be sent at once to replace the governor of the province of Africa and finish off Jugurtha as quickly as possible. Marius's arrival, along with volunteer reinforcements from the *proletarii* (the lowest social class of Rome), gave the campaign the impetus it needed. The war swiftly came to an end, and Numidia was made safe for the equites to start their business dealings there once more.

WAR WITH THE CIMBRI AND THE TEUTONES, 104 B.C.

The war with Jugurtha had proved no threat to Rome's security. However, almost immediately after it ended, a real danger arose. A Roman army in Cisalpine Gaul was defeated by migrating German tribes, the Cimbri and the Teutones. An invasion of Italy seemed imminent, and in 104 B.C. Marius again was elected consul, and again he was immediately given an army command, this time in Cisalpine Gaul. For the second time the people had disregarded the Senate's right to appoint generals to provincial commands, and also had ignored the rule forbidding anyone to hold a second consulship within ten years. In fact, as the war with the German tribes continued in the north, Marius was to be elected consul for three more successive terms—and the Senate's protests each time were quieted by the treat of mob violence, ruthlessly stirred up by a crony of Marius, the tribune Saturninus.

The advance of the Cimbri and Teutones was slowly checked, and they finally were driven out of Roman territory in 102 B.C. as a result of Marius's great victory at Aquae Sextiae (present-day Aix-en-Provence). The people believed that he had saved Rome from the Germans as surely as Camillus had saved it from the Gauls nearly three hundred years earlier. Marius, hugely popular, returned to Rome and was rewarded with a *triumph*. This was a celebratory parade, only on rare occasions voted by the Senate for a general who had particularly distinguished himself. It was always an honor greatly sought after. The victorious army would march through the streets of the city, with prisoners and booty on display, trumpets and flutes playing, and the general bringing up the rear in his chariot.

By 100 B.C., Rome again seemed safe, and Marius was elected consul for the sixth time. Once more the mobs were brought out by Saturninus. They forced the Senate to approve Marius's foundation of colonies and grants of land for his veterans—and this time the soldiers themselves joined in the riots. But then Saturninus, running for election to another tribunate, openly had his opponent murdered. Alarmed, the Senate passed the *senatus consultum ultimum* against him. Marius, acting as a conscientious consul, and no doubt worried in any case that he had lost control of Saturninus, was now forced to repudiate him.

What happened to Saturninus is not known, but his supporters were rousted out and punished with a firm hand. Though Marius had allowed the people to stand up for him against the Senate when he had sought military commands, he had no political ambitions, and was not willing to defend mob behavior. With calm more or less restored in Rome, he retired to his house in the country.

MARIUS'S ARMY REFORMS

Marius's military victories had been won in part because of his own stubborn leadership by example, but owed even more to his radical reorganization of the Roman army. During the years of his army commands, he ended the old system of drafting recruits for the duration of a war and then demobilizing them to fend for themselves. In its place he established a professional standing army, open to all, even those in the lowest class. The legion, comprised of 6,000 men at full strength, was subdivided into smaller units for greater flexibility. The smallest unit was the century of one hundred men, under a centurion, an experienced, hardened leader who had risen through the ranks, unlike the raw young officers from the aristocracy, whose service too often had been regarded as simply the first stage in a career in politics and who often were appointed as a favor to their fathers. The centurions now formed the unflappable core of every Roman army.

The infantry were for the first time uniformly equipped and armed; the traditional short jabbing sword remained unchanged, but the *pilum* (throwing spear) was modified with a point that broke off on contact (so that it could not be thrown back), or stuck inside the victim (so that it could not be pulled out). The soldiers also had to carry their own entrenching tools, so that their camps could be properly fortified with a ditch and a rampart. On the march with their kits on their backs, they were popularly known as *muli Mariani* (Marius's mules).

In addition, each legion was given a *signum* or standard (from which the English word *ensign* is derived). The standards were long poles topped by decorative attachments—the number of the legion, the letters SPQR surrounded by a laurel wreath, and a bronze *aquila* (eagle). These served as regimental colors, a symbol of the legion's identity and morale, as well as a highly visible mark round which the men could rally during battle. The standards were closely guarded, and if one was lost or captured, the legion and the general were thought to be disgraced—as badly, perhaps, as if they had been captured themselves.

Marius's army reforms were extremely successful in improving fighting effectiveness, mobility, and morale, but there were political dangers built into them. The new professional soldiers came mostly from the most underprivileged class of society, which had little feelings of loyalty to a state that seemed to have ignored them. They felt

IX.1 Modern drawing: officers confer in front of the general's tent. Note the differing types of standard. (Bettmann Archive)

instead that they were fighting for the general who had recruited them. After all, it was the general who arranged for their pay—which came mainly in the form of cash bonuses and shares of booty from captured towns and enemy armies—and it was the general who had to bring pressure on the Senate after every campaign to make the allotments of farmland that were the only pensions the veterans received. The Senate seems to have felt no responsibility for the welfare of Rome's armies, and since Marius had set the precedent of encouraging the people, rather than the Senate, to choose who should command the army in each province, many generals no longer felt a commitment to the Senate.

Reading

Marius' Greatness Foretold (Plutarch: *Lives*, Marius 3)

Marius's parents were quite unknown and quite poor. They made their living from what they produced for themselves on their farm. . . . Most of his youth was spent in the countryside of Arpinum; life there was unsophisticated and uncomplicated compared with the luxurious style of Rome—and it was more like the straightforward simplicity of the old days.

Marius first served in the army in Spain under Scipio [the grandson of the conqueror of Hannibal, and the general who had destroyed Carthage in 146 B.C.]. . . . He was noticed by his general because of his courage, and because he had not complained when discipline was tightened up in reaction to the soldiers' self-indulgent habits. There is a story too that he had beaten an enemy in single combat while his general was watching. He was well rewarded for his feat; and later, at a dinner party, when the conversation turned to the topic of leadership . . . somebody asked Scipio where the Romans would find another general such as himself. And Scipio put his arm round Marius, who was sitting next to him, and said, "Perhaps this is your man."

Chapter Ten

SULLA

THE ITALIAN WAR (THE SOCIAL WAR), 90 B.C.

*T*en years after Marius's retirement, Marcus Livius Drusus again raised a question that had been discussed since the time of the Gracchi: citizenship (including the vote) for Rome's Italian allies. Neither the Senate nor the people had ever been enthusiastic about such an idea. The Senate felt that it would lose whatever control it still maintained over the deliberations of the assembly, if members of the assembly came from still more varied backgrounds and whose points of view and demands could be less easily anticipated or satisfied. The people of Rome, on the other hand, feared that they would receive smaller rations of cheap grain if it had to be shared among a larger body of citizens. For these reasons, earlier proposals to give the vote to the Italian allies had failed, even when the allies themselves increasingly complained that they were asked to fight for Rome but had no Roman rights. However, when Drusus was assassinated in 90 B.C., and yet another opportunity for receiving citizenship seemed to have been lost, the Italians rose in open revolt.

As was usual in most of their wars, things went badly for the Romans at the beginning. The Italians were mostly experienced soldiers, and their leaders had organized them well. However, in 89 B.C. their headquarters were captured by an officer called Lucius Cornelius Sulla, and their resistance began to falter. Even so, the fighting continued fiercely in some places, and in order to save lives and also to recognize the justice of the Italians' cause, the Senate advised the tribunes to propose the first of a series of laws that eventually granted the Italians full Roman citizenship.

Rome was now no longer a city, but a nation. The inhabitants of Italy still lived in their own towns under their local governments, but now they were also Romans, with the right to involve themselves in the affairs of the Roman republic, and to embrace the opportunities and privileges Rome offered its citizens. In practice, of course, the Italians seldom found their way to Rome to exercise their vote; nor could they slow the gradual degeneration of the assembly into an irresponsible mob, a process which had been going on for the past hundred years. Moreover, it would be a long time before a system of local polling places was set up, and before the Italians actually became magistrates or members of the Senate.

SULLA'S RISE TO POWER

Because he had captured the Italians' base, Sulla wished the people to believe that he had single-handedly ended the Italian War. Indeed, it was his habit to claim credit whether or not it was deserved. Earlier, as a junior cavalry officer in Numidia, Sulla had argued that he, not Marius, was responsible for Jugurtha's defeat. If psychiatrists had existed, they might have diagnosed him as suffering from an inferiority complex—and certainly Sulla's background gave him reason to feel inferior. Though of a noble family, he had grown up poor and neglected. He had inherited money from a Greek prostitute, who had been his father's favorite mistress. He had a purple birthmark on his face that his critics said made him look like "a mulberry sprinkled with meal." Yet his military performance had been impressive enough to get him elected praetor in 93 B.C. and consul in 88 B.C.—a year in which Rome was faced with another foreign crisis.

While the Romans were distracted by their wars against the Germans and the Italians, in the East the ambitious Mithridates, King of Pontus, had tried to extend his kingdom by invading the Roman province of Asia. He pushed aside light Roman resistance there, and then gained the support of the people by telling them they no longer had to pay taxes to Rome. Then he conceived a plot to rid the province of its Roman residents, mainly merchants and their families. In a carefully concerted coup, 80,000 Romans were massacred in a single night—a slaughter known as "the Asiatic vespers." To meet this crisis, Sulla, now ending his consulship, was appointed governor of the province of Asia, with a mandate to stop the forces of Mithridates, who was now preparing to advance into Greece.

But when Sulla arrived at Brundisium and was preparing to sail with his army across the Adriatic, a tribune suddenly proposed that the command be given instead to Marius. The suggestion was absurd as well as illegal. Marius had not seen military action for more than ten years. He had played no part in the Italian War, and was now in his late sixties. Outraged by the tribune's action, Sulla easily persuaded his army to march with him back to Rome and to seize control of the city—triggering the first of the series of civil wars that Rome was to suffer during the next half-century. At Sulla's instigation, Marius was driven into exile with a price on his head, and Sulla then returned to Brundisium and set sail for Greece.

Meanwhile, Marius had gone into hiding, taking refuge in peasants' cottages and in the marshes south of Rome, then fleeing to Sicily and Africa. However, as soon as Marius heard that Sulla was safely out of the country, he foolishly allowed his friends to persuade him to return to Rome. He was swept along in part by his own rash subordinates, in part by the memory of a fortune-teller who in his childhood had foretold that he would be consul seven times. Marius finally reentered the city, and he had many of Sulla's supporters murdered. They were mainly members of the senatorial class, for Sulla had always been too proud to ingratiate himself with the people. Now Marius was granted his seventh consulship, but the excitement—or the guilt—was too much for him, and he died a few days later. Cinna, the remaining consul, maintained control of the city by raising troops against the return of Sulla.

SULLA AS DICTATOR, 82–79 B.C.

Cinna did not have to wait long. After two decisive battles, Sulla had compelled Mithridates to negotiate a peace. Because he was in a hurry to get back to Rome, Sulla's terms were lenient: simply that Mithridates had to withdraw from the territory he had overrun. Sulla, however, did not disband his soldiers. Instead, he brought them back with him into Italy, where they were reinforced by three legions enlisted there on his behalf by a young lieutenant called Gnaeus Pompeius (usually anglicized as Pompey). After a full-scale battle just outside the city, the battle of the Colline Gate, Rome was again captured by Sulla, and Pompey dealt with minor pockets of resistance from Marius's supporters in Sicily. For this service, Sulla gave Pompey, perhaps sarcastically, the title of Magnus (the Great).

The Senate, relieved to see a lull in the storm, but apprehensive of future confusion and chaos, extended Sulla's *imperium* by appointing him dictator in 83 B.C.—not, however, a dictator of the old-fashioned temporary kind that had been last used in the war against Hannibal. Instead, Sulla was made dictator with an indefinite term of office, with the specific task of "restoring the republic." Nevertheless, Sulla's first order of business was to acquire land for his veterans, and this he did by a program of "proscriptions." Under this program, Sulla posted in the forum lists of his opponents whom he wished to be rid of. Those whose names were on the lists were liable to be murdered without reprisal if they stayed in Rome, and whether they did or not, their property was confiscated. Since many of them were equites, Sulla's pickings were rich.

Sulla then proceeded with his reforms, which were mainly intended to strengthen the Senate. He increased the numbers of the Senate from three hundred to six hundred, to include some of the equites who had stayed loyal to him as well as some of the more prosperous of the new Italian citizens. All ex-magistrates now were automatically to become Senate members, so that the people could feel that they had a hand in determining the membership of the Senate, and would thus be less likely to question its authority. He also reestablished the Senate as the jury of the permanent law-courts, and as his most lasting achievement, he reorganized the entire system of criminal justice.

Sulla's other new laws were meant to prevent future civil wars and in fact, they forbade many of the very actions he and Marius had taken to gain power. He strictly enforced the rules of the *cursus honorum*, including the age limits for each office, and forbade the reelection of anyone to the same office within ten years. He attempted to tighten the Senate's control over the provincial commands by insisting that the Senate could never allow the choice of governor for any province to be made by any body except the Senate. In particular, it now became illegal for a governor to leave his province, or lead his troops outside it, without the Senate's permission.

Sulla's dictatorship lasted little more than three years, and in 79 B.C. he resigned and went to live on his country estate. The reasons for this action are not clear. He may have feared assassination by his enemies, who suspected that the dictator had plans to make himself king. On the other hand, he may have thought, like Solon in Athens, that if his new constitution was sound, it would be able to function without his immediate authority. Or he simply may have felt old and tired and sick. After a few months away from Rome, he died.

Reading

The Dangers of Being Rich (Plutarch: *Lives*, Sulla 31)

Without any consultation with the magistrates, Sulla immediately proscribed eighty people. A storm of protest did not prevent him, two days later, from proscribing a hundred and twenty more, and as many again on the day after that. In a speech to the assembly, he announced that he had dealt with as

X.1 Wall painting: luxurious country houses, a tempting target for anyone wishing to get rich from the proscriptions of Sulla. (Bettmann Archive)

many people as he could think of, but the names of anyone that he had forgotten would be published later. In addition, he said that he would proscribe anyone who aided or abetted someone who had already been listed—and that included brothers, sons, and parents. Two talents' reward was offered to anyone who killed a man whose name was on the lists, even if a slave were to murder his master or a son his father. . . .

Proscriptions took place not only in Rome, but also in the Italian countryside. Nowhere was there a safe haven—not the sanctuary of a temple, not a private house. Men were stabbed in their wives' arms, children in their mothers'. Some died because they were considered a danger to the state, others because they were personally disliked by the dictator—but the great majority met their end simply because they were rich. Even those who actually did the killing began to say that it was really a man's house, or his garden, or his private baths, that had done him in.

Chapter Eleven

POMPEY, CRASSUS, AND CICERO

POMPEY IN SPAIN

*W*hen Sulla's regulations were broken for the first time, it was the Senate itself that was responsible. By showing himself indispensable as Sulla's aide in 83 B.C., Pompey had put himself into the Senate's good graces, and in 76 B.C. he was appointed proconsul in Spain, although he never before had held an office of any kind. The Senate instructed him to get rid of Sertorius, a former lieutenant of Marius who had protested against what he considered Sulla's illegal dictatorship and had recently stirred up a revolt in Spain. Pompey eventually put down the rebellion, but only with great difficulty, and he succeeded largely because Sertorius himself was assassinated. However, Pompey did somehow manage to keep himself in the public eye as a popular and promising general.

SPARTACUS AND THE SLAVES' REVOLT, 72 B.C.

Sertorius was not the only thorn in the Roman side. In 72 B.C. the slaves on the *latifundia* revolted, led by a gladiator from Greece named Spartacus. He was apparently an organizer of genius, and he became a cult figure in the twentieth century in the Soviet Union as the first man to call upon the workers of the world to unite. Spartacus formed the slaves into a disciplined army of seventy thousand, with a base on the slopes of Mount Vesuvius, about a hundred miles south of the city.

Most of the rebellious slaves were from Gaul, and Spartacus's original plan was to lead them north until they could go home. The consuls attempted to cut them off, but the slaves were victorious in a half-dozen battles. In the end, however, they were trapped and rounded up by Marcus Crassus, a banker who had made himself enormously rich during Sulla's proscriptions by helping himself to other people's money. However, Spartacus's revolt was not entirely without result: it led to a definite improvement in the conditions on the *latifundia*, though the price was high. Spartacus was killed, and six thousand captured slaves were crucified along the length of the Appian Way, in order to discourage future rebellions.

POMPEY IN THE EAST

Pompey returned from Spain in time to mop up the last survivors of the fleeing slaves, and infuriated Crassus by announcing that he had defeated them by himself. For a moment it looked as if they might actually go to war with each other. However, they decided instead to bury their differences and stand together for the consulship of 70 B.C. In fact technically neither man was eligible for the office: Crassus was a year too young, and Pompey still had never held office in Rome. But when both of them refused to disband their armies, the Senate nervously allowed the election and Pompey was voted a triumph. The manner in which they gained office clearly demonstrated that Sulla's reforms were already dead. Once in office, their achievements as consuls were negligible. In fact, the major event of the year 70 B.C. was the trial of Verres, a corrupt, unprincipled governor of Sicily, who was prosecuted by one of Pompey's admirers, Marcus Tullius Cicero.

Cicero was a *novus homo* at the outset of his career, looking anxiously for the approval of the people. After winning his case against Verres, Cicero spoke out energetically in favor of two measures that were to give Pompey his first real power. The public was growing impatient with the recent activities of pirates in the Mediterranean. These pirates were boarding Roman merchant ships, attacking Roman naval units, and disrupting the grain supply from Africa; they had even landed on the Italian coast and kidnapped a couple of senators who were walking on the beach. Actions by provincial governors had been entirely ineffective. Finally, in 67 B.C. a tribune had the assembly of the people push through a bill (the *lex Gabinia*) that gave Pompey unrestricted *imperium*, without time limit, to end the pirate threat. In a brilliantly coordinated naval campaign, Pompey wiped them out in a single summer.

The next year, in 66 B.C., another tribune had passed the *lex Manilia*, giving Pompey similar powers against Mithridates, who again was causing serious trouble in the eastern provinces. Pompey took over from Lucullus, the governor of Cilicia, who was equally well-known for his delicious dinner parties and for his ability to defeat Mithridates's armies regularly without getting rid of Mithridates. Again displaying brilliant strategy, Pompey forced Mithridates to retreat inside a fortified city, and laid siege to him there until he committed suicide.

But Pompey was not yet finished in Asia. He now set out to consolidate Rome's power in the East so that nuisances of this kind could not occur there again. He rewrote the terms of the treaties of alliance with the remaining Hellenistic monarchs to guarantee Rome a ring of client-kingdoms as a buffer against the Parthian empire, which comprised most of the territory of modern Iraq and Iran. New towns were to be founded to take care of those who had been dispossessed by Mithridates. Mithridates's kingdom of Pontus was to become the province of Bithynia, and Syria also was to become a province. The taxes from Bithynia and Syria would nearly double Rome's income from its provinces, and also would provide pensions for Pompey's retired soldiers. By these proposals (called his "Eastern settlement"), Pompey had shown himself a great administrator as well as a great soldier. With supreme confidence he laid his proposals before the Senate for their ratification.

Reading

An Influential Woman (Plutarch: *Lives*, Lucullus 19)

At that moment word came that the governor of Cilicia had died, and a great many men who wanted his job came to see Cethegus, who was known as the best man to arrange such things. Lucullus was most anxious that he and no one else should obtain the post, because, although Cilicia was of no importance in itself, it was the province from which a war might be launched against Mithridates. . . .

Now Cethegus had a mistress whose name was Praecia; she was famous for her wit and her looks, but she was in fact nothing more than a prostitute. . . . She had seduced Cethegus, the most influential man in Rome, and then saw to it that anyone who wanted to see Cethegus would have to arrange an interview through her: as Cethegus had a hand in anything that anyone else did, so Praecia had a hand in anything that Cethegus did. So Lucullus gave her expensive presents and flattered her—and frankly it was a real comedown for her, so splendid and elegant a figure had she now become, to be seen in association with Lucullus—and thus he soon contrived to become friendly with Cethegus; and he persuaded Cethegus to make the appropriate arrangements to ensure that the governorship of Cilicia should be given to him. In the end he was unanimously voted into the office, and after that he did not have to talk with Cethegus or with Praecia anymore.

CICERO'S CONSULSHIP AND CATILINE'S CONSPIRACY, 63 B.C.

On his return to Rome in 63 B.C., Pompey found that there were two small flies in the ointment of his satisfaction. First, Crassus still resented Pompey's role in the Slaves' Revolt and now was openly jealous of his Eastern success, muttering vague insinuations about Pompey's regal ambitions. Secondly, Cicero, now consul, was contriving to upstage Pompey by representing himself as *Pater Patriae* (the Father of his Country). Cicero made this claim because he had successfully ended a conspiracy to take over the state by Catiline, a disgruntled young

XI.1 Nineteenth century painting by Cesari Maccari: "Cicero and Catiline in the Senate." (Art Resource)

nsuccessfully run against Cicero for the consulship.
ed details of the plot from an informer, and at the
ıad pounced. Catiline was killed and the rest of the
ᵉ arrested and put to death. Cicero himself made
uncement of their fate to the people: *"Vixerunt!"*
nished.)
ıcy in fact had been poorly planned and had no chance
remembered only because of Cicero's impassioned
Catiline in the Senate. Cicero, however, was con-
ı saved the state from populist anarchy, and he began
to restore the old republican ideals. He tried to per-
conflicting parties in Rome to forget their differences
ᵓrdia or *consensus* of "all good men." It was a roman-
ᵗeam—even the senators would not take him seri-
was a *novus homo*—but Cicero probably lost his
ᵗortant political career by refusing to abandon it.

Chapter Twelve

THE FIRST TRIUMVIRATE

THE BEGINNING OF THE TRIUMVIRATE, 59 B.C.

*F*ar more serious than the posturings of Crassus and Cicero, however, were the actions and attitude of the Senate, which to Pompey's bitter disappointment, began, for no apparent reason, to carp at the details of his Eastern settlement, and then refused to ratify it. Pompey now looked round for others who might wish to join him in forcing the Senate's hand. He remembered a former admirer of his, Gaius Julius Caesar, a noble who was also connected by marriage with the humbler Marius, and who had been a partner with Crassus in dubious financial dealings, which he had used to pay off his debts. Caesar had already been praetor and was now the governor of Farther Spain, where he had enjoyed some military success putting down yet another rebellion. However, he was having difficulty in extracting from the Senate both the promise of a triumph, and also permission to stand for the consulship of 59 B.C. *in absentia*—for, as governor, Caesar was not allowed to leave his province—with the guarantee of another provincial command afterward.

Caesar therefore willingly agreed to ally himself with Pompey, and to seal the deal Pompey married Caesar's daughter Julia. Along with Caesar came Crassus, who presumably decided that it was safer to be with Pompey than against him. The three of them formed what they called simply an *amicitia* (friendship)—though it is known to historians as the First Triumvirate. It was an informal, quite unconstitutional pact, whose members shamelessly threatened to use force if the Senate did not give them what they wanted. Cicero was asked to join, but refused; this kind of action had nothing to do with his ideal of *consensus*.

In 59 B.C., the Senate caved in before the triumvirate's pressure. Caesar was allowed to run for the consulship and was duly elected. He ignored the protests of his fellow consul—cynics called his term "the consulship of Julius and Caesar"—and smartly put through the measures the triumvirate had demanded: the ratification of Pompey's Eastern settlement, with grants of land to his veterans; changes in the laws of Asia that benefited Crassus's equestrian friends; and for himself a special five-year command in Cisalpine Gaul, where he had recognized a tempting opportunity for his personal ambition.

At the end of his year as consul, Caesar went off to his provincial command in Gaul as planned, leaving the tribune Clodius to look after his interests in Rome and to keep an eye on Pompey. However, Clodius's idea of carrying out Caesar's instructions was to quarrel with another tribune, Milo, who supported Pompey. Both Clodius and Milo organized gangs of professional agitators who rioted in the streets of Rome on command and achieved nothing except Cicero's banishment (for putting to death the Catilinarian conspirators without a trial) and then, in the very next year, his recall. Acutely embarrassed, Pompey avoided the city, and contented himself with criticizing Crassus.

Reading

Young Ambition (Plutarch: *Lives*, Julius Caesar 11)

It is said that one day, when Caesar was a very young man in Spain, he was spending a day off-duty in reading a biography of Alexander the Great. Then he looked up from his book and sat lost in thought; and finally he started to sob. His friends asked him what the matter was. "It's enough to make anyone cry," he said. "Look at how many countries Alexander had already conquered at my age—and so far I have done nothing worthwhile at all."

CAESAR IN GAUL, 58–50 B.C.

On the other side of the Alps, the Gauls had requested help from the Romans in settling a border dispute with a migrating tribe from Switzerland. Caesar was happy to answer this call, because it was important for the Romans to maintain control over the roads and passes between Italy and Spain. However, he had no intention of returning to his province once he had dealt with the problem. Instead, Caesar conceived a grand plan to conquer all the tribes of Gaul and he moved steadily northward—probably the first truly imperialistic enterprise of Roman history.

The detailed story of Caesar's campaigns is told in his own account, the *Bellum Gallicum* (Gallic War). In this memoir he describes how he divided and conquered the enemy by swift forced marches in all directions across the countryside and by achieving dashing military victories. (There is a plain in northwest France where alignments of prehistoric monoliths are still said by local residents to be one of Caesar's legions turned to stone.) Later, some tribes in northern Gaul revolted and had to be reconquered. Since the rebel tribes had used Britain as a base for recruiting and training their forces, Caesar decided to invade Britain in 55 B.C. However, he was beaten back by the blue-painted natives and by the British weather, losing many of his ships because he did not understand the action of the tides in the English Channel. When peace was finally restored, in 50 B.C., he divided the whole of Gaul into several provinces, including Gallia Comata (long-haired Gaul) and Transalpine Gaul (Gaul on the other side of the Alps), now called Provence. The subsequent Roman presence in Gaul, which lasted for over five hundred years, laid the foundations of modern France and Belgium.

Reading

Druids in Gaul (Caesar: *The Gallic War*, vi.16)

The lives of the Gauls are entirely bound up in their religion, and for this reason those who are suffering from serious diseases and those who are threatened by some danger, or who are going off to war, either offer up other men as sacrificial victims or promise themselves at a later date. And they ask the Druids to take proper charge of these sacrifices, because they think that the gods will only be satisfied if they receive another man's life in exchange for their own.

There are also public sacrifices of the same kind. Sometimes the Gauls will construct a statue of enormous size made of intertwined vines; they then fill the arms and legs with living men, and set the whole thing on fire, so that the men perish in the flames. They think that the sacrifice of those who have been caught pilfering, or in any other antisocial behavior, is particularly welcomed by the immortal gods. But if there is a shortage of criminals, then they will have recourse to sacrificing the innocent instead.

THE END OF THE TRIUMVIRATE, 49 B.C.

In the middle of his Gallic campaign, Caesar had to return briefly to Italy to meet with Crassus and Pompey to try to patch up their relations—which had become strained as a result of the machinations of Clodius and Milo—and to make arrangements for the future. It was decided that Caesar's command was to be extended to 50 B.C., and it was arranged that Crassus and Pompey would be consuls for 55 B.C. In the following year, Pompey contrived to become governor *in absentia* of both Roman provinces in Spain. This meant that technically he had command of the armies there, though he was permitted to remain in Rome. Crassus, in turn, received the glamorous military command he had always wanted; he was sent to Syria to make war on the Parthians. At the battle of Carrhae in 53 B.C., Crassus's army was soundly defeated, his eagles standards were captured, and he himself was killed. The Parthians celebrated by staging a vulgar pageant in which they poked fun at Crassus's effeminate manner. Fortunately for Rome, however, they did not follow up on their victory. Crassus's death was followed immediately by that of Julia (Caesar's daughter who had married Pompey), who died in childbirth. The last tie between the two surviving triumvirs was broken. Now both of them, motivated only by personal ambition, schemed to bring about the other's downfall.

In 53 B.C., more rioting broke out in Rome between the gangs of Clodius and Milo, and no consuls were elected. The following year, the Senate began to panic at the prospect of Caesar's return, and they put Pompey into office as sole consul. The Senate then accused Caesar of a double crime against the state: using force to put through measures during his consulship in 59 B.C., and illegally extending his provincial command. Pompey was embarrassed as well as gratified at seeing his rival under fire, for he had originally condoned and encouraged both of these actions. Moreover, if he was to criticize Caesar too loudly, Pompey's own highly irregular position as absentee governor of Spain might come under scrutiny. He did not know what to do, and so he did nothing.

Caesar also faced a dilemma. If he returned to Rome without his troops, he would at once be impeached by a jury of senators—and that would surely mean the end of his career. But if he brought his troops with him, he would be breaking Sulla's law, still technically in force,

XII.1 Portrait bust of Pompey the Great. "Truly remarkable only in his ambition for power."—Sallust (Bettmann Archive)

which forbade a general to lead his army outside the boundaries of his province. Thus, Caesar would be committing an act of civil war. Neither Caesar nor Pompey wanted war, but at the same time neither was willing to sacrifice his ambition for the sake of a principle. After they had rejected various proposals for mutual disarmament, and with negotiations at a stalemate, at the beginning of 49 B.C., the Senate passed its *consultum ultimum,* and instructed Pompey to take up arms against Caesar if Caesar did not disarm unilaterally. On the banks of the Rubicon, the river that marked the boundary between Cisalpine Gaul and Italy, Caesar hesitated for three days more. Finally, on January 10, he declared, *"Alea iacta est"* (The die is cast), and entered Italy at the head of his legions.

Reading

An Apparition on the Banks of the Rubicon (Suetonius: Lives of the Twelve Caesars, Julius Caesar 31)

At once Caesar secretly sent ahead a detachment of troops; but he himself went to the theatre, inspected the site of a proposed school for gladiators, and gave a dinner party, all in order to allay suspicion that anything unusual was afoot. But after dark

XII.2 Infantrymen at ease before going on duty. (Art Resource)

he requisitioned a pair of mules and a cart . . . and set off with his lieutenants toward the frontier. Their lights blew out and they got hopelessly lost . . . but at dawn they met a peasant who took them on foot through the back lanes until he could once more set them upon their right road. Caesar came up to his troops on the bank of the Rubicon, which marks the boundary between Gaul and Italy. . . .

He stood, still hesitating, on the bank; and then he saw a human figure, larger than life and eerily beautiful, playing on a reed pipe and surrounded by a group of shepherds and some of Caesar's soldiers who had drifted away from their formation. Suddenly the figure snatched a trumpet from a soldier, blew a call and moved across the river. "It is a sign from the gods," said Caesar. "Let us follow where he leads, to take vengeance on those who have betrayed us."

Chapter Thirteen

JULIUS CAESAR

CIVIL WAR: POMPEY VERSUS CAESAR, 49–46 B.C.

*P*ompey had hoped that the population of Italy would spontaneously rise up to oppose Caesar and his approaching army. When this did not happen, Pompey determined that Italy should not again become a battlefield and that any fighting would take place abroad. With the consuls and all the Senate, he evacuated Rome and set sail from Brundisium for Greece. There, with an army collected from the province of Syria, Pompey awaited Caesar's pursuit. Caesar followed him at the head of his own loyal troops, and decisively defeated Pompey's forces at the battle of Pharsalus. Looking at the dead bodies—mostly senators and nobles—Caesar commented sadly, *"Hoc voluerunt"* (This is what they wanted). Caesar's words reflected his own belief that he had been forced into the war against his will—and that his victory was not a triumph but a tragedy.

However, the war was not yet over. The rest of Pompey's army retreated, along a giant circle around the Mediterranean, and suffered defeats in Egypt, in Syria—where, after the battle of Zela in 47 B.C., Caesar coined his most famous phrase: *"Veni vidi vici"* (I came, I saw, I conquered)—and in Spain. But fairly early in the Civil War, Pompey met his own end in Egypt. As he came ashore in Alexandria he was stabbed by agents of fifteen-year-old King Ptolemy XIII, who thought to do Caesar a favor. Pompey's head and ring were sent to Caesar, who wept when he saw them; he and Pompey had once been friends, and he had never expected their feud to end like this.

Egypt at this time was involved in its own civil war between the supporters of Ptolemy and those of his elder sister Cleopatra. The two were supposed to be joint-rulers, and, as was the custom in the Egyptian royal family, they had married each other. They were not Egyptians, but rather Macedonians, the direct descendants of one of Alexander's generals, and imbued with Greek rather than African ideas. Although Caesar's troops were drawn briefly into the fighting, the main casualties of the war were the great library at Alexandria, which accidentally went up in flames, and Caesar's heart, which he lost to Cleopatra. She soon became his mistress, and when the war ended he set her up in style in Rome, much to the disapproval of the Romans, who—whatever their private predilections—were prudes where their leaders were concerned.

THE DICTATORSHIP OF JULIUS CAESAR, 46–44 B.C.

In 46 B.C., what was left of the Senate welcomed Caesar when he returned to Italy and at once elected him dictator (as it had Sulla earlier), to reestablish order in the state. Caesar's wartime lieutenant, Marcus Antonius (Mark Antony) became his official assistant, or *magister equitum*. Unlike Sulla, however, Caesar did not execute or exile Pompey's supporters—not even Cicero, who had been particularly hostile to him before the Civil War.

As dictator, Caesar's aim was not to put into practice any political theory of his own. Instead, his purpose was to make the existing system efficient. However, where institutions of the republic had shown themselves inefficient, he stripped them of their power. He enlarged the Senate to nine hundred to replace the members killed during the fighting and included enough Italians to make it truly representative of the whole state. Yet Caesar took over the Senate's responsibility for finance, foreign policy, and the disposition of provincial commands. In these matters he only went through the motions of consulting the Senate.

By controlling the elections, Caesar made certain, too, that he got the magistrates he wanted. In particular, he made sure that he himself was annually elected as one of the two consuls, even while he remained dictator. Once he assured himself of the loyalty of the army by a large increase in its pay, he had no fear of rivals.

For the civilian population of Rome, he paved roads and opened another forum. He drained a large area of marsh outside the city to provide more agricultural land. He started construction of a new Senate House to replace the one burnt down by Clodius's mobs. All this was expensive, and it was paid for by heavy fines on the towns in Spain and Asia that had supported Pompey's cause, and by the *portoria*, a tax on goods entering or leaving Italian harbors.

Caesar made wide grants of citizenship to provincials outside Italy, including all the men in his favorite twentieth legion, "the Lark," which he had recruited in Gaul. He also established more than twenty Roman colonies overseas for his own veterans and for some of Rome's urban poor. In this way Caesar consciously encouraged the spread of Roman institutions and culture throughout the Mediterranean and the Middle East.

One of Caesar's most important changes was his reform of the old Etruscan calendar used by Rome. This system had gone out of synchronization with the solar year, even though two extra months (January and February) had been introduced during the early republic so that September had become the ninth rather than the seventh month. Caesar borrowed most of his new calendar from the Egyptians, but he also added extra days to some months and introduced leap year. (In a moment of self-congratulation he renamed the seventh month Julius.) With minor changes made by Pope Gregory XIII in 1582, Caesar's calendar is still in use in the West today.

THE ASSASSINATION OF CAESAR, 44 B.C.

There was little about Caesar's reforms which could be criticized because they were not useful or because they did not work; but there was considerable anxiety regarding Caesar's own future role in the government of Rome. For all those who admired Caesar for what he had achieved, there were others who felt he had moved too fast, and without proper respect for people's feelings or Rome's tradition. And, in truth, Caesar often seemed cold and distant, nor did he suffer fools gladly—and arrogance can easily be mistaken for unhealthy ambition. In the Senate especially, though members for the sake of peace and quiet had acquiesced to Caesar's drastic removal of their responsibilities, many did not believe their acquiescence should mean perpetual subservience to Caesar. They agreed with Cicero, who wrote that Caesar "was prepared, for the sake of power, to ignore all that was right and good." And as they heard what Caesar said with his lips, they began to wonder what he intended in his heart.

Increasingly the old question was now asked by the oligarchs, as it had been asked before about Gaius Gracchus, Sulla, and Pompey: did Caesar mean to make himself king? There was no doubt that he had allowed his portrait to appear on coins, and that he had raised no

XIII.1 Nineteenth century engraving: Julius Caesar as dictator, in his scarlet general's cloak. (Bettmann Archive)

objection to the founding of a religious cult around himself, in imitation of the practice in the Hellenistic kingdoms. Republican eyebrows were raised, too, at Cleopatra's rumored wish to be queen of Rome as well as of Egypt, at Caesar's wearing of a purple robe, and at Mark Antony's offering him a crown at a public festival. Was Antony joking? If so, it was a joke in extraordinarily bad taste. Certainly, like Sulla, Caesar saw the Senate as backward-looking and out of date, incapable of dealing with the ever-changing complexities of the empire. And he certainly considered Sulla foolish to have voluntarily resigned his dictatorship. But equally certainly Caesar was annoyed if the title of "king" were used of him: "*Non sum rex*, he grumbled, "*sed Caesar.*" (I am Caesar, not a king.)

For a few senators, led by Gaius Cassius and by Marcus Brutus—
who could not forget he was descended from that Brutus who had been
one of the first two consuls in 509 B.C.—the time for asking questions
was over. They had whispered conversations in public places, they held
agitated meetings in private houses, and at last their minds were made
up: Caesar must go.

If Caesar heard any word of the plot, he would not admit to fearing
it. He refused a bodyguard, he refused to alter his daily routines, he
refused to take notice of warnings or omens. He even told his friends
that he wanted a quick and unexpected death. On the Ides (15th) of
March in 44 B.C., he went to preside at a meeting of the Senate at the
theatre built by his defeated rival Pompey. (Caesar's new Senate House
was not yet finished.) In the middle of the morning's business, he was
surrounded by twenty-three conspirators and stabbed twenty-three
times. As he fell, he looked straight into Brutus's eyes—Brutus, who
despite their differences was his old friend. Then his blood splashed up
over Pompey's statue. Caesar was dead.

XIII.2 Portrait bust of Marcus Brutus. "This was the noblest Roman of them all."—
Shakespeare (Bettmann Archive)

Readings

The Loyalty of Brutus's Wife (Plutarch: *Lives*, Brutus 13)

Brutus [anxious about the progress of the conspirators' plan to murder Caesar] tried to keep his worries to himself and to keep calm; but at home he was fidgety and irritable, and kept on waking suddenly in the night . . . so that his wife could not help noticing that something was very wrong and that he was tormented by a serious problem.

Portia had been married to Brutus when she was very young. . . . She was deeply interested in philosophy and at the same time loved her husband very much. She vowed that she would not try to share Brutus's difficulties until she had demonstrated to herself that she could keep a secret. When she was alone, she took a knife of the kind using for paring nails, and cut herself deeply in the thigh. She lost a great deal of blood, and suffered considerable pain with a high fever.

Brutus became worried about her health, and at last she said to him: "I am your wife; I have promised not just to share your bed but also your whole life, in sickness and in health. . . . How can I return your love for me if I cannot share your sorrows, if you will not tell me anything which requires you to rely on my integrity? I know that most people think that women are incapable of keeping a secret, but I am of noble birth, I was well educated, I have known many honorable men—and these things have left their mark on me. . . . Now I have given myself a test, and have shown myself that I can bear pain in secret."

Then she showed him her wound, and explained what she had done. . . . And Brutus prayed the gods that he might show himself a worthy husband to her.

The Ides of March (Plutarch: *Lives*, Julius Caesar 63)

Many strange omens and signs appeared before Caesar's murder. Apart from shooting stars, noises in the night, and wild birds which settled on the buildings of the Forum—events that might normally not be thought to give information about the fate of important personages—there was a display of soldiers, fighting with each other in the sky and glowing with an incandescent light. Another soldier had his hand burst into flames—although afterward, contrary to all expectation, there was no trace of any injury. An animal that was being sacrificed by

Caesar was discovered to be missing its heart—a very bad sign indeed, because without a heart nothing can stay alive. It was also widely rumored that Caesar was warned of a great danger that would threaten him on the Ides of March; and on that very day, on his way to the meeting of the Senate, he met the man who had warned him. "The Ides of March have come," he said, jokingly. But the answer came with great seriousness: "Yes, they have come, but they have not yet gone."

Compare the following scenes from *Julius Caesar* by Shakespeare, who used much of Plutarch's account as his model:

Act I, scene ii:
Caesar: Who is it in the press that calls on me?
   I hear a tongue, shriller than all the music,
   Cry, "Caesar!" Speak: Caesar is turn'd to hear.
Soothsayer: Beware the Ides of March.
Caesar: What man is that?
Brutus: A soothsayer bids you beware the Ides of March.
Caesar: Set him before me; let me see his face . . .
   What say'st thou to me now? Speak once again.
Soothsayer: Beware the Ides of March.
Caesar: He is a dreamer; let us leave him; pass.

Act II, scene ii:
Calpurnia: Caesar, I never stood on ceremonies,
   Yet now they fright me. There is one within,
   Besides the things that we have heard and seen,
   Recounts most horrid things seen by the watch.
   A lioness hath whelped in the streets;
   And graves have yawn'd, and yielded up their dead;
   Fierce fiery warriors fought upon the clouds
   In ranks and squadrons and right form of war,
   Which drizzled blood upon the capitol;
   The noise of battle hurtled in the air,
   Horse did neigh, and dying men did groan,
   And Ghosts did shriek and squeal about the streets . . .
Caesar: What say the augurers?
Servant: They would not have you to stir forth today.
   Plucking the entrails of an offering forth,
   They could not find a heart within the beast.

Act III, scene i:
Caesar [to the soothsayer]: The Ides of March are come.
Soothsayer: Aye, Caesar, but not gone.

Chapter Fourteen

THE SECOND
TRIUMVIRATE

ANTONY TAKES CHARGE

*A*t the moment of his assassination, Caesar had been simultaneously consul and dictator; thus he was survived by Mark Antony, his colleague in the consulship, and by Lepidus, his current *magister equitum*. Lepidus had just been appointed governor of Gaul, and he and his army were on the point of leaving Rome. To prevent any public demonstrations, and perhaps to secure his own safety, Lepidus occupied the forum. But Antony, who wanted no troops in Rome unless he was in charge of them, managed to persuade Lepidus to depart at once for Gaul.

Mark Antony then acted with great energy and dispatch. To calm the apprehensions of Caesar's supporters among the people, he sensibly announced that all Caesar's laws would remain in force. Equally sensibly, he soothed the republicans by abolishing the office of dictator, and granting an official amnesty to the conspirators. But he could not allow Caesar's death to appear to go unavenged. Therefore, he summoned the people to the assembly, where by parading Caesar's bloody body and by reading Caesar's will—which purported to leave a small sum to every Roman citizen—he provoked a riot against the conspirators, so that they fled the city. At the same time Antony made sure that he himself did not lose the conspirators' favor by arranging with the Senate that Brutus and Cassius should be given provinces in the East, where they found armies who were loyal to them.

85

For the moment, Antony had achieved what he wanted: He had been able to prevent the conspirators from immediately restoring the republic; he had presented himself as Caesar's successor, though a moderate one; and he now was clearly in command.

THE ARRIVAL OF OCTAVIAN

Antony may have forged that part of Caesar's will that he had read to the people, but he could not change the reality of Caesar's heir, his grandnephew Octavian, now an eighteen-year-old university student in Greece, who had come to Rome as soon as he learned of Caesar's death, and who also had paid a courtesy visit to Cicero as senior republican. Though he did not fully trust Octavian, Cicero was sufficiently impressed and flattered to make a series of speeches—now called the *Philippics*, after Demosthenes's tirades against Philip II, the father of Alexander the Great—in which he attacked Antony with ever increasing violence. Antony was entirely unscrupulous, he said; he was another Caesar, only worse; and the Senate should give its full support to Octavian if only to get rid of Antony.

Meanwhile Antony was finding it impossible to pin down Octavian's intentions. Octavian, though very young and very skinny, was a good deal tougher than he looked. They argued about Caesar's money —Antony seems to have embezzled some fairly substantial sums—and about each other's political standing. When Octavian raised an army from among Caesar's old soldiers, Antony accused Octavian of plotting to assassinate him. Then fighting broke out, and Antony fled to Gaul, where Lepidus gave him his support. Octavian, even though he was not yet twenty, now used his troops to get himself elected to the consulship of 43 B.C. The Senate became alarmed at the imminent prospect of yet more war. Therefore it brought together Antony, Lepidus, and Octavian, and passed a bill (the *lex Titia*) that formally instructed the three of them to take joint control of the state (in an association later called the Second Triumvirate).

Reading

Cicero Attacks Mark Antony (Cicero: *Philippic*, ii.25,45)

Your acts against the law at least showed some signs of energy. But enough of them—let me now speak rather of your acts of trivial thoughtlessness. At Hippias's wedding you succeeded in drinking so much—sucking the stuff down your great throat, using your gladiator's lungs and muscles—that the next day you were sick in full view of the Roman people. It was not only horrible to see it then, it is horrible even to hear about it now. Bad enough if it had happened at a private dinner, after you had been chugging from one of those enormous mugs that you own. But you were the *magister equitum*; you were on official business before the assembly of the Roman people. When even a belch would have been out of place, you vomited up chunks of food still stinking of wine, first into your lap and then all over the speaker's platform. . . .

I beg you, Antony, to consider the future of the republic. Think, too, not only of those who are alive today, but of your ancestors. As far as I personally am concerned, what you do is your own business; but for your sake, you should return to the embraces of your fatherland.

However, you have made your bed. Now I shall speak for myself. When I was a young man I fought for the republic; I will not desert her now that I am old. If I thought nothing of Catiline's sword, shall I be scared by yours? I would be glad to give up my life, if by my death freedom could be restored to my country.

THE SECOND TRIUMVIRATE

The Second Triumvirate was very different from the first. The first had been an entirely unofficial group, formed by its members with the intention of putting persuasive pressure on the Senate. The second, however, was the result of a legal enactment, formally proposed by the Senate, which gave its three members unlimited power in war and peace, at home and abroad. In effect, the Senate had exercised its own authority to vote itself and the republic out of existence.

The first act of this triple dictatorship—though the word was avoided by all the parties—was to follow the example of Sulla in drawing up proscriptions to get rid of its enemies. The most famous victim was Cicero, for Antony had not forgotten the *Philippics*. It was a sad irony that Cicero, the Roman republic's greatest champion of moderation, conciliation, and the peaceful settlement of differences, should meet his death by despotic violence. (The eighteenth-century romantic Horace Walpole might have been thinking of Cicero when he wrote: "No country was ever saved by good men, for they will not go to the lengths that may be necessary.") But the proscriptions damaged Octavian, too: history has never forgiven him for his part in these pointless murders. Though he may genuinely have wished to avenge Caesar,

Octavian might also have remembered that Caesar was famous for his clemency.

Having made it clear that they would allow no opposition, the triumvirs now began to nominate magistrates to serve in Italy and the provinces, while they also divided the western provinces among themselves. Their immediate business, however, was to raise an army to take revenge on Caesar's assassins. For this they needed money, and thus for the first time Roman citizens were to be directly taxed. Leaving Lepidus at home in case of trouble, Octavian and Antony crossed into Greece, and defeated the armies of Brutus and Cassius at two battles, both at Philippi. These victories left dead most of the aristocrats who might have offered any opposition to Octavian. Brutus and Cassius themselves committed suicide in the traditional Roman way, by running onto swords held by their slaves.

OCTAVIAN AND AGRIPPA

After the battles of Philippi in 42 B.C., the triumvirate broke up. Lepidus, who could not make up his mind whether to be ambitious or phlegmatic, was sent off into early retirement; Antony stayed in the East, and Octavian returned to Rome.

Comets and other auspicious omens welcomed Octavian. The poet Vergil even wrote an ode in which he forecast the birth of a mysterious child who would rule over a new Golden Age. Yet the immediate reality was harsh. Octavian himself was regarded with some suspicion as a newcomer to the scene, and many Romans still preferred Antony's more cheerful, down-to-earth manner. Despite Caesar's projects, much of Italy's countryside and the city of Rome was run-down or neglected. There were food riots; many veterans had to be settled by unpopular confiscations of land; and Pompey's son, Sextus, had raised an armed revolt on Sicily, calling himself a second Neptune. To restore order would have been a daunting job for an experienced administrator, whereas Octavian was still in his early twenties. Nevertheless, though it took him nearly ten years of pushing and pulling, of threats and promises, Octavian proved successful. Throughout these difficult years, he was buoyed by the faithful service of Marcus Agrippa, who became his closest friend and ally. Agrippa's energy in war, especially in his campaigns at sea, made up for Octavian's lack of military expertise. Sextus Pompeius finally was defeated in 36 B.C. after Agrippa had built a new fleet and trained sailors to man them. As aedile, Agrippa was able to boost Octavian's popularity with the people by undertaking an ambitious program of reconstruction in Rome, by cleaning up the city's water supply, and by expanding the distribution of cheap wheat.

XIV.1 Formal portrait of Cleopatra, wearing the crown of Egypt, and holding the insignia of her office. (Bettmann Archive)

ANTONY AND CLEOPATRA

While Octavian was busy in Italy, Antony, who liked soldiering much better than politics, was enjoying himself in Macedonia, where he easily subdued rebellious tribesmen from the north, and in Syria, where he fought the invading Parthians. After several years of fighting, the Parthians were driven back (though with heavy Roman losses) and a new client-kingdom, Armenia, was enrolled to protect the boundaries of the empire in the east. But these military campaigns cost money, and to beg, borrow, or steal it, Antony decided to go to Egypt, where Cleopatra was back on the throne, having been ignominiously smuggled out of Rome after Caesar's assassination.

Antony had met Cleopatra before, when he had accompanied Caesar to Egypt during the Civil War, and he remembered her well. Captivated just like Caesar, Antony soon became her lover. Cleopatra, however, was clever—fully as clever as Antony—and she ruthlessly used her feminine wiles to get fair return for the money that she decided to give him. Antony was trapped. He promised on his own initiative to make gifts of large parts of Roman provinces to her, to her son by Caesar, Caesarion, and to their own twin children, to whom they had given the splendid names of Alexander the Sun and Cleopatra the Moon. The news of these so-called "Alexandrian donations" caused a sensation in Rome as well as among Antony's own troops. For his part, Antony apparently had no idea what offense his alliance with the Egyptian queen would cause.

Apart from his anger at the arbitrary distribution of Roman territory, Octavian was particularly bitter about Antony's affair with Cleopatra because Antony, in an attempt to smooth over the awkwardnesses which had developed between them since the dissolution of the second triumvirate, had recently married Octavian's sister, Octavia. Thus, Octavian's family honor was insulted, and he was probably additionally sanctimonious because he himself had just gotten married—for the second time—to Livia, an aristocratic divorcée with two small sons.

Public opinion now made it easy for Octavian to rally support against Antony, and finally to secure his own position. In 32 B.C., the population of Italy took an oath of allegiance—probably voluntarily—to Octavian. This declaration of support gave Octavian both the confidence and the popular mandate he needed, and he declared war—technically on Cleopatra, but in reality on Antony.

XIV.2 Livia at the time of her marriage to Octavian. (Bettmann Archive)

Hostilities were quick and anticlimactic. Antony advanced into Greece with Cleopatra at his side, but Octavian's army remained in Italy. In a preliminary maneuver, Agrippa tried to lure Antony and Cleopatra into a naval engagement off the west coast of Greece at Actium. But the moment Agrippa's new fleet appeared on the horizon, Cleopatra's ships put about and fled back to Egypt. Without her naval contingent, Antony's ships were greatly outnumbered, and he followed her without a backward glance. The following year, both committed suicide in Alexandria within a few months of each other, Antony by stabbing himself, Cleopatra by allowing herself to be bitten by a viper. Octavian had Caesarion murdered, but spared most of Antony's lieutenants. He canceled the Alexandrian donations, confiscated the Egyptian treasury to pay his soldiers, and annexed Egypt as a special province in his personal possession.

As a battle, Actium was a nonevent, yet its result may have changed the history of the world. Octavian was now left unopposed as the sole and absolute ruler of Rome. Agrippa had brought him victory in war; now he must establish a lasting peace.

Readings

The Tricks of Cleopatra (Plutarch: Lives, Mark Antony 29,53)

Plato says that there are four types of flattery, but Cleopatra had mastered a thousand. It made no difference whether Antony was in a serious or a silly mood, she always had some delightful trick to capture his attention; she was always with him, and did not let him out of her sight by day or night. She played dice with him, she drank with him, she went hunting with him; she would watch him when he was in the field on military exercises. . . .

One day Antony was fishing with Cleopatra, and while she was there he had no luck. So he quietly ordered a fisherman to dive down and hook onto the end of his line some fish which had already been caught. But when he pulled in his "catch," Cleopatra spotted what was going on. However, she pretended to be overcome with admiration and proudly announced what a great angler Antony was. "You must come and see him," she told everyone. So a crowd assembled on Antony's boat; but when he made his cast, one of Cleopatra's slaves got at his hook before Antony's man could, and fastened onto it a fish from Bithynia, already cooked and salted. Antony felt the movement on his line, and hauled it in. When they saw what he had snagged, everyone roared with laughter, and Cleopatra said, "Fishing is a sport better left for the monarchs of poor old Egypt—you should stick to catching cities and provinces and kingdoms."

. . . On hearing that Antony's wife Octavia was planning to meet him, Cleopatra became uneasy. She was afraid that Antony might be seduced into a more serious and permanent attachment to his wife if she was always at his side, affectionate, attentive, and as elegant as her way of life and her aristocratic breeding could make her. So she pretended to be dying of love for Antony; she made herself thin by rigorous dieting, she never took her eyes off him when he came into the room, and she pretended to faint when he left it. She made sure that he noticed her crying—and then, when she saw that he had noticed her, she dried her tears and turned her face away from him as though she had not wanted him to notice. . . . Her slaves were quick to play supporting roles in this drama: they let Antony know that they thought him heartless and insensitive, because he was allowing a woman who had become entirely dependent on him to pine away from love of him. . . . At last she undermined his resolve completely and convinced him that if he left her she would die; so he changed his plans and returned to Alexandria.

The Battle of Actium (Vergil: *Aeneid*, viii. 672)

The sea froths with white wave-caps, and dolphins beat upon the surface with their tails as they dip and dive. In the middle you can see the bronze beaks of the fleets in battle formation, reflected in the glittering waves. Here Augustus [i.e., Octavian] leads all Italy to war—gods great and small, senators and people. He stands on the high poopdeck, flames playing round his temples and Caesar's star above his head. Alongside him the untiring Agrippa leads another column, favored by the gods and by the winds; on his head is a crown, made to look as though it is formed of the prows of battleships. And opposite, rich with foreign gold and foreign allies, the conqueror of the East and of the Red Sea, is Antony, followed by his Egyptian wife, of whom no Roman should ever even speak.

PART III The Empire

Chapter Fifteen

THE PRINCIPATE OF AUGUSTUS

THE ROMAN EMPIRE IS FOUNDED

Since the formation of the Second Triumvirate in 43 B.C., the republican constitution, and popular freedom, had been officially ended. Now Rome under the autocracy of Octavian would come back to life in a brand-new form. Though Octavian claimed merely to have restored the republic, posterity has not been misled, and today his arrangement is conventionally known as "the Roman Empire" (with a capital E), and its rulers as "emperors."

Octavian himself, however, chose to refer to himself as *Princeps* rather than *Imperator*. He intended this word to distract attention from his real powers, and to imply that he was simply the "first citizen" or "first among equals"; it also happened to be the title of the senior member of the Senate, thus giving it a comforting old-fashioned ring. Octavian also was addressed by his *cognomen* Caesar, inherited through his great-uncle's family. This family name would later become the generic title for all subsequent Roman emperors, whether or not they were related to Octavian. From it come the German word *Kaiser* and the Russian *Tsar*. In 27 B.C. the Senate, in a decree meant only to flatter him, gave to Octavian his own *cognomen* of Augustus, the name by which he hereafter was always known. In Latin this word means "revered," but being derived from the Etruscan word *augur* (an interpreter of omens), it also had religious significance, suggesting that the

93

gods took pleasure in this new position. Later the Senate, in further acts of flattery, renamed the eighth month after Augustus and awarded him the ultimate title of *Pater Patriae.*

ORGANIZATION AND ADMINISTRATION OF THE EMPIRE

Toward the end of his life, Augustus wrote an autobiographical survey of his principate called *Res Gestae* (What I Have Done). It is a valuable historical source, as long as one remembers that it also is self-serving propaganda and omits anything that might be subject to negative criticism. In it Augustus claimed that he had "given the republic back to the Senate and people," and that he had always acted according to the *mos maiorum.* Though far from the truth, the Romans liked the sound of these words, because they always had been nervous about change in

XV.1 Bronze statue in Rome, dedicated "by the Senate and People of Rome to the Emperor Caesar Augustus, the son of a god, the father of his country." (Bettmann Archive)

their institutions, and they still shied away from anything that connoted "king."

Whatever his private determination, Augustus certainly intended that the new empire appear to be governed jointly by the emperor and the Senate. In fact, the Senate chose not to use even the power that Augustus gave it, and instead turned its discussions with him into fawning, silent acts of obedience. The frank and impassioned speeches that for so long had been a mark of senatorial debate were no longer admired; and the Roman tradition of oratory soon died out. Only the courts of law remained the Senate's prerogative, and even there an appeal to the emperor rather than to the people was allowed.

Technically, however, Augustus's power was indeed held by the advice and consent of the Senate. Every year the Senate allowed him to be solemnly reelected consul, and colleagues were even elected with him. This went on till 23 B.C., when he was given permanent proconsular *imperium*. But much more important than the consulship was his simultaneous, permanent takeover of the power of the tribune. As tribune, Augustus could convene the Senate and also propose legislation—always of course under the safe assumption that it would be approved and passed. And as a crucial safeguard, he had the tribune's veto. But beyond any constitutional office, Augustus possessed the force of his own character, his expectation that he would be obeyed without question, his personal *auctoritas* (authority, or prestige). It was a larger, more personal form of the prestige that the Senate had possessed in the time of the Punic Wars, derived not from law, but from respect.

Though the Senate had lost its power and transferred its prestige to the emperor, its members still did not deign to work in a trade or for pay. Thus when Augustus decided to institute a professional civil service, he turned to the equites, and he used freedmen to perform most of the empire's clerical work. Administration throughout the empire became noticeably more efficient, and misrule in the provinces became rarer. Equites were also appointed to serve as financial officers in the new imperial provinces, as the emperor's deputies in Egypt, and to supervise the imperial grain supply. Equites commanded the fleets and the emperor's bodyguard, the praetorian guard; they also took charge of Rome's first fire brigade—originally a force of six hundred slaves, later of freedmen—and of its first police force, which helped deter riots but could do little to prevent endemic crime in the streets.

AUGUSTUS STRENGTHENS THE EMPIRE

The single most important lesson Augustus had learned from the civil wars was that independent action by ambitious generals operating out of their provinces must be forestalled. Marius, Sulla, Pompey, and Caesar all had secured political power by such means. Augustus therefore divided the provinces into two groups: an outer "imperial" ring, which was to be governed by himself, and an interior "senatorial" ring, governed in the traditional way by pro-magistrates. Troops were to be stationed only in the imperial provinces, under the emperor's direct control and commanded by generals whom he appointed. The troops were to be paid from the treasury rather than by the emperor himself, with money raised from death duties and a sales tax.

Under Augustus, the empire was enlarged slightly, mainly to shore up gaps in its defense system. The buffer client-kingdoms also were strengthened. The right to make foreign policy, like everything else, was silently ceded by the Senate to Augustus. And his foreign policy was a simple one: to keep the empire as far as possible within its existing boundaries.

In the North, campaigns were fought against the German tribes— a border war directed by Drusus and Tiberius, the emperor's stepsons —and once more in the East, against Parthia. In Germany, Roman standards were lost by the general Varus to a German chieftain—a disaster which shamed Augustus ever afterwards. However, in Parthia

XV.2 Cameo celebrating the religious cult of *Augustus et Roma*. Below, Roman soldiers round up prisoners of war. (Bettmann Archive)

the Romans recovered the standards captured from Crassus at the battle of Carrhae, and a peace treaty was signed with the Parthians, allowing Roman merchants to pass through India into China, where they traded for silk. Throughout the East the religious cult of *Augustus et Roma* was encouraged in order to satisfy the local peoples accustomed to worship their kings as gods; in return many Eastern cults were introduced into Rome by returning soldiers.

There was much unrest in Syria, and also to the south in Judaea (a client kingdom ruled by king Herod till his death in 6 A.D., and then a separate province). Internal squabbling broke out between the local sects, and anti-Roman sentiment increased, especially among the Jews. But despite such sentiment, Augustus extended his policy of religious toleration to the Jews: they were exempt from military service and no portrait of the emperor appeared on their coins, in deference to their opposition to "graven images."

About the middle of his reign, Augustus required that a census be taken throughout all the provinces for the purpose of assessing taxes. From Syria, where Quirinius was governor, the count apparently was extended into Judaea. At one census point in the village of Bethlehem, more people gathered than could find proper lodging for the night. In a makeshift shelter, a woman went into labor, and the child who was born there was called Jesus.

Readings

The Emperor's View of Himself (Augustus: Res Gestae 2, 34)

According to the judgment of legally established courts, I sent into exile those who had murdered my father, and I avenged their crime. Afterwards they made war on the republic, and I defeated them in two battles.

I made war by land and sea all over the world against enemies from within and without. I conquered them all; and to everyone who asked for mercy, I gave it.

In my sixth and seventh consulships, after I had brought to an end all the civil wars, after I had gained complete control, and after I had gained universal support, I transferred the power to make all decisions concerning the republic out of my own hands and back to the Senate and people of Rome. And for this action the Senate decreed that I should be called Augustus; that the doorposts of my house should be wreathed with laurel, and that a garland should be fixed over my door. . . . After this time I was superior to everyone else in my authority, but I had in fact no more power than those others who were my colleagues in the magistracies.

Though—with the approval of the Senate and people of Rome—I was appointed guardian of public laws and morals, to act by myself and with supreme power, I accepted no office unless it was consistent with the customs of our ancestors.

A Poet's View of the Emperor (Horace: *Odes*, iii.3)

A man who has justice in his heart and is unbending in his purpose can never be swayed by the insistence of citizens who urge him to do what is not right. . . . Even if the whole world collapse about him, still he will stand unafraid among the ruins.

By unassailable resolve such as this, Pollux and the wandering Hercules came after long struggles to the heights of starry Olympus; and there, lying back on his couch with a bright shining face, already drinking nectar among the immortal gods, is Augustus himself.

An Historian's View of the Emperor (Tacitus: *Annals*, i.2)

Gradually Augustus swept aside all opposition, taking to himself the functions of the Senate, the magistrates, the lawgivers. Anyone who had any spirit of independence in him was dead, as the result of war or execution. Those who were left behind found that if they did exactly what they were told, they would do well in politics or in business. They had already done well out of the civil wars, and for them it was better to be safe under the new arrangements than sorry under the old ones.

WEAKNESSES OF THE PRINCIPATE

The principate, Augustus's new system of government for the empire, was efficient enough, but even with the new equestrian civil service, administration was an enormous task, requiring the emperor's own skilled hand on the tiller at all times. Augustus had provided for almost every contingency except the incompetence of future emperors; he also had not foreseen the decline in public morals that would come about when the task of government was concentrated in the emperor's hands.

With few official duties or responsibilities, many of the nobles now gave themselves over to acquiring the luxuries that foreign trade and overseas contacts offered them—to competitive and conspicuous consumption. The egregious vices of the Romans were almost entirely the vices of the aristocrats; though they were not necessarily the only ones who could afford the orgies, the banquets lavish to the point of obscenity, and the Oriental dancing girls, they were the only ones who had the leisure to enjoy them. But even the nobles' wealth was not inexhaustible. Though they wanted ever more expensive pleasures, at the same time they did not want to be forced to sell off their land in order to afford them; consequently, corruption and usury flourished among them. Their crimes and their excesses were a frequent topic for contemporary historians and satirists, who took a high moral tone but were unable to resist a scandal.

The trends that had begun to undermine Roman family life after the Punic Wars continued: more celibacy, more divorce, and more re-marriage. Marriage, particularly among the rich, had become little more than a convention to produce an heir; it often served as an instrument to pursue politics by other means, to join together influential families or individuals. For political reasons, Pompey had married Cae-sar's daughter, and Antony had married Octavia; Augustus made his own daughter Julia marry three different men, one after the other, to further his own purposes. And not surprisingly, the emperor's attempts to legislate morality proved futile. Sumptuary laws against excessive spending, laws against adultery, tax breaks for married men—none of this legislation had any effect on the rising tide of self-indulgence and frivolity.

More serious critics of the Principate might also have complained of the diminished political role of the people. In turn, Augustus might with equal force have argued that the people did not deserve such a role. For nearly two hundred years now, the people had ceased to be the cool-headed, equal partners of the Senate, willing to listen to reason and rational debate. They gradually had lost such power as the consti-tution had given them and had become the instrument first of well-intentioned reformers like the Gracchi and later of unprincipled rabble-rousers like Saturninus, Clodius, and Milo. Moreover, the people showed no sign of wanting their freedom back. The equites were fully occupied with their profitable business connections and the civil service bureau-cracy; the middle classes were content to work in their market stalls, their workshops, and on their farms, enjoying the peaceful times Au-gustus had brought them; and the urban *proletarii* accepted poverty and unemployment as long as they had their *panem et circenses* (bread and circuses).

Readings

An Iconoclast's View of the Games
(Pliny the Younger, *Letters*, ix)

I spent all this time writing and reading—it was a most delightful period of peace and quiet. "How could you spend your time like that in the city?" you may ask. It was a day when the games were being held—a spectacle in which I am not even remotely interested. There's nothing new, nothing different, nothing which would be worth seeing even once. I wonder how so many thousands of adults can behave like children—watching horses running about and men standing in chariots behind them.

If they were interested in the speed of the horses or the skill of the drivers, I could understand it. But they support one team or another only because of their team colors; it's the colors that they get so excited about. If, in the course of a race, one team's colors were switched with another's, the crowd's enthusiasm and support would be switched too, and they would abandon the drivers and the horses that just before they had been cheering on.

A Banquet in the Early Empire (Petronius: *Cena Trimalchionis*, 40)

Meanwhile slaves had come in and spread blankets on our couches, embroidered with scenes of men lying in wait with spears and nets and all manner of hunting equipment. We were still wondering what would happen next, when a fearful racket sprang up outside the dining room, and in burst a pack of great hounds which began to circle the table. After them a boar of enormous size was borne in on a salver; he had a cap on his head like the ones that freed slaves wear, with two baskets suspended from his tusks, filled with various kinds of dates.

Then, to carve the boar, came forward not the fellow who had sliced up the chickens that we had eaten for the first course, but a gigantic man with a beard, tricked out in a fancy tunic with an unsheathed hunting knife in his hand; he slashed fiercely at the boar's flank, and straightaway a flock of thrushes flew out from the cut that he had made. Birdcatchers were standing by with snares; in a flash they grabbed up the thrushes as they tried to fly about the room. Our host ordered a thrush to be presented to each guest, and then he announced:

"Now let's see if that wild pig hasn't eaten an elegant acorn."
And at once the slaves went up to the baskets which hung from
the boar's tusks, and divided out the dates equally among us.

THE PROBLEM OF SUCCESSION

Many Romans must have wished—or even believed—that Augustus
would live forever, but he knew well that he was mortal, and fairly
early in his reign he began to plan for his successor. Augustus's personal pride as well as republican tradition suggested that the next
princeps should be a member of his own family. But any candidate
must first prove his energy and competence, and then be clearly designated. Finally, at the appropriate moment, the Senate could go through
the formal procedure of confirming and electing him to the office. It
was a wise policy, and it was not Augustus's fault that it did not work
out as he had hoped.

To start with, Augustus had no son of his own, only a daughter by
his first marriage, Julia. But his sister Octavia, before she had married
Antony, had had a son, Marcellus, by a previous marriage, and Augustus's eye fell first on him. Marcellus's early public appearances
made him popular with the Roman people. He was conveniently married to his cousin Julia, and was duly praised by the poet Vergil. Unfortunately, after having demonstrated nothing but promise, he died of a
fever (probably malaria) in 19 B.C. Augustus's next choice, made with
excellent good sense, was his old friend Agrippa.

Agrippa had felt all along that he should be considered, and had
been openly jealous of Marcellus. But now Agrippa was given the power
of a tribune and he was made governor of the Eastern imperial provinces so that he should be well experienced in the ways of the Principate if the worst should happen. Augustus brought Agrippa into his
own family by two routes: he officially adopted him as his son, and
then also had him marry his daughter Julia, though she was barely
recovered from Marcellus's death. The marriage presented certain
problems. Julia was only eighteen and Agrippa was forty-two; moreover, they were quite different in personality, and when Julia began to
run with wild friends her own age, Agrippa was deeply embarrassed.
Then in 12 B.C. Agrippa died, leaving Julia with no less than five children from their seven years of unhappy marriage. The two oldest were
two boys, Lucius and Gaius. Augustus was delighted with his grand-
sons, who grew into bright and charming teenagers, and either of them,
he thought, might very well do as his heir. He made both of them
consul when they reached the age of twenty and sent them off to serve
in provinces. Unfortunately, they both died abroad, one of fever in
4 B.C. and the other of wounds in 2 B.C.

XV.3 Cameo portrait of Livia with her son Tiberius, who was later to become the second Roman emperor. (Museum of Fine Arts, Boston)

There was now left only Augustus's stepson, Tiberius, who was Livia's son by her previous marriage to a crusty Roman noble of the old school. Tiberius was now in his late forties. As a young man, he had been happily married to Vipsania, Agrippa's daughter. But after Agrippa's death, Augustus had forced him to divorce her and marry poor Julia, who had already become simultaneously his step-mother-in-law and his step-sister. Tiberius hated Julia, who was now so demoralized by this third marriage of convenience that her private behavior became a public scandal. As punishment, in 2 B.C. Augustus vindictively banished her to a small island off Naples, and gave instructions that he never again wished to hear her name mentioned.

It was no wonder that Tiberius was sour and disillusioned. He had loved his first wife, but she had been taken away from him; his second wife had disgraced him; he had enjoyed soldiering against the German tribes, but he had no desire to be emperor, especially since he obviously was his stepfather's last choice. Nevertheless, in A.D. 4, with the Senate's consent, he was given the tribune's power and the same *imperium* as Augustus. Thus for the next ten years he was virtually co-emperor with Augustus, and he was formally adopted as Augustus's son.

Only Livia seemed completely pleased. The talk in Rome was that Tiberius's accession was what she had wanted all along, and that the death of so many of Augustus's previously designated heirs had not necessarily been natural or even accidental.

Chapter Sixteen

ART NOT FOR ART'S SAKE

*A*ugust's Principate was more than a triumph of organization and administration. Despite criticism that he had substituted despotism for democracy—flawed though the democracy had been—Augustus gave a free hand to artists and writers, commissioning many projects himself. His encouragement of the arts was not, of course, entirely altruistic. Augustus was a master of propaganda and many of the works of his reign were deliberately conceived to glorify the emperor's position and his achievements. Art and politics were particularly well coordinated under the patronage of Maecenas, Augustus's closest friend after Agrippa. Maecenas was most influential in his support of new writers, and assiduously bought the work of new artists for his luxurious house in Rome. Although he never held political office, he advised the emperor constantly and kept him informed of useful new talent.

ART AND ARCHITECTURE

The art of the Romans, like everything else in their culture, was a construction of other people's ideas, modified by their own requirements. Roman sculptors were enormously influenced by the Greeks, as might be expected. The richest Romans collected original Greek statues, especially those of the fifth and fourth centuries B.C., either buying them or, like Verres the governor of Sicily, appropriating them. But a far larger number, who could not find or afford originals, were happy to possess reproductions, and an entire industry grew up in Rome of copying them. When originals have been lost, it is common to find that copies have survived. It is certainly possible to tell one from the other, but at the same time the copiers' workmanship and attention to detail was admirable.

The chief characteristic of classical Greek sculpture was its idealism; the Greeks represented human figures as they thought they should be rather than as they are. However, Roman artists were also interested in realistic portraits. Many examples of these portraits that have survived on Roman coins and in busts show what many famous figures of history really looked like, warts and all. But the effect sometimes seemed odd when the two styles were combined in a single statue, for example, when a Roman portrait head, of a venerable, wrinkled statesman, was attached to a beautifully muscled and proportioned young body of the Greek ideal type.

Perhaps the most successful example of Roman sculpture can be seen on the *Ara Pacis* (the altar of peace), dedicated by the Senate to celebrate Augustus's safe return in 9 B.C. from a tour of Gaul and Spain. The sides of the altar bear, in relief, figures of magistrates and priests leading sacrificial animals in a religious procession, all framed by elaborate decorative swags of fruit and flowers.

The Romans copied the Greeks in the design of their country houses and their large town houses; they passed hot air through terra-

XVI.1 Modern reconstruction of the Ara Pacis. (Art Resource)

XVI.2 An aqueduct, built to carry water from the mountains into the city of Rome
(Bettmann Archive)

cotta pipes below the floor to heat them, and decorated the inner
rooms with frescoes of landscapes and mythological scenes in the
Etruscan fashion. In their temples, too, they often followed the standard Greek model, but frequently with the addition of extra stories
below and above. However, the Romans varied the appearance of the
exterior colonnade by using Corinthian columns, which the Greeks
had used only for interior decoration. In addition, Roman architects
improved on the Greek and Egyptian *pylon*—two columns and a lintel,
shaped like the letter *pi*—as a method of spanning a space. The Roman
arch, modified over the years from an original Etruscan invention, was
stronger and more versatile than the pylon. And as usual when the
Romans adapted ideas from abroad, the results were peculiarly their
own. They used the arch in various combinations to build aqueducts
and viaducts across valleys, and they developed the dome and the barrel
vault—called a *basilica* when it appears in a large building such as a
law court, a shopping arcade, or a temple.

At the end of his life, Augustus boasted that he had "found Rome
built of brick and left it of marble." In his ambitious program of public
works his motive was perhaps the same as that of Pericles when he
rebuilt the temples on the Acropolis of Athens. Not only did the construction of glittering new temples, baths, and theatres in Rome provide jobs for the poor, it also inspired an appropriate sense of awe and
civic pride among the Romans themselves as well as visitors from the
provinces or foreign countries.

Yet there was another face of the city behind the ostentatious public buildings. Its most characteristic feature was the blocks of tenement houses, called *insulae* (islands), where large numbers of people lived. These *insulae* were several stories high, because it was cheaper to build upward than side by side in the limited space available. Usually the *insulae* contained shops on the ground floor and apartments above. They were designed in an unimaginative cubelike form (similar in appearance to many modern urban project-houses), and were poorly constructed of brick and wood. When concrete came into general use, they became more solid, but still remained dark, overcrowded, and unsafe. Fires were common—despite Augustus's institution of a fire brigade—and destructive.

The streets in front of the *insulae* were not much better. Away from the *fora* and the splendid approaches to the emperor's palace and the Senate House, they were narrow and noisy, unlit at night and clogged with traffic by day. The droppings of hundreds of mules and horses were smelly and attracted insects, especially malaria-bearing mosquitoes from the marshes (which, for all their efforts, the Romans never succeeded in properly draining). And yet Rome under Augustus was still a most exciting and habitable city—it was, after all, as one of his poets said, the capital of the whole world.

LATIN LITERATURE'S "GOLDEN AGE"

The end of the Roman republic and the years of Augustus's Principate, like the second half of the fifth century in Athens, was one of those short periods in history where an unusually large number of unusually gifted writers suddenly burst together into notice. It is hard to say what the stimulus may have been. Most of the great works of Athenian literature were composed in wartime, sometimes when Athens was winning, sometimes when it was losing and demoralized. In Rome, too, some of the best Latin writers flourished in times of civil disturbance and uncertainty, some in the years of stability that followed.

The Prose of Cicero and Caesar

Cicero probably thought that his life's greatest achievement was his consulship of 63 B.C. and his rescue of Rome from Catiline's conspiracy, but posterity knows better. The fact is that Cicero is one of those rare figures more admired for what they said than for what they did. Cicero's failure to achieve his political ends has not taken away from his enormous skill as an orator. He was a lawyer before he became a politician, and the texts of more than fifty of his speeches in the courts and before the Senate have been preserved because—as was the fashion —he wrote them down after their delivery and had them published. His mastery of calm, reasoned argument, of invective, of sly irony and vicious sarcasm, make him a model for public speakers even today. Most memorable were his speeches against Verres, the corrupt governor of Sicily, against Catiline, and the *Philippics*, his attacks on Mark Antony of 44 B.C.

Cicero also was an addicted letter writer. He wrote to his friends, to his brother Quintus, who was also murdered in the proscriptions of the Second Triumvirate, and to his brother-in-law Atticus. He wrote in detail on daily affairs in Rome, as well as about family matters. These letters provide a touching look at his private feelings, and they are a valuable source for historians of the final years of the republic. During Caesar's dictatorship Cicero was not in office; he withdrew from public life for a period of eighteen months. At home, in his study, he wrote poetry (what has survived is pretty bad) and a large number of philosophical essays—partly as an interpretation of Plato and Aristotle, partly as an exposition of his own Stoic beliefs. In contrast to the fury of his speeches, these meditations are soothing and peaceful, and their themes are still worthy of consideration. He wrote on *Old Age*, for instance, and *Friendship*, and the moral *Duties* of a citizen.

While Cicero was writing philosophy, Julius Caesar was dashing off "Commentaries" on his two most important campaigns, the *Gallic War* and the *Civil War* with Pompey. The "Commentaries," which he intended to polish into formal histories during his retirement, are actually first drafts; their Latin is usually simple and direct, but the expression is sometimes awkward and occasional sentences are of immense length. The *Gallic War* used to be widely read by students as their first taste of "real Latin"; it since has lost popularity because of its overlong, detailed recital of route-marches and countless skirmishes and battles, yet it contains much interesting material on the customs of the Gauls.

Lyric Poetry: Catullus, Horace, and Ovid

The Romans based their poetry on Greek models, both with regard to theme and meter. One of the earliest and most passionate of the Greek lyric poets was Sappho, who was imitated closely by Catullus, the most passionate of Roman poets. Catullus was born in Cisalpine Gaul where his father was governor during the dictatorship of Sulla. He lived most of his life in Rome, where he fell in love with Clodia, the sister of Clodius, who had led the riots against Milo in 58 B.C. Clodia was about ten years older than Catullus and had a bad reputation—she was suspected of murdering her husband and of committing incest with her brother. Catullus's affair with Clodia did not go smoothly; most of his poetry was a desperate plea for her affection, as she alternately spurned him and led him on. The poems are composed using Greek lyric meters as far as possible, but their passion prevents them from being mere imitations. In a complimentary reference to Sappho, Catullus refers always to Clodia as "Lesbia," and indeed one of his most famous works is a translation into Latin of one of Sappho's poems. In another poem he shows that despite his anguish he had kept his sense of humor: he addresses Lesbia's pet sparrow, who is allowed to hop about on her body in all the places where Catullus wishes he, too, might be permitted.

Readings

Poem to Lesbia, Translated from the Greek (Catullus: *Poems,* 51)

He seems to me to be equal to the gods,
And—if I may say such a thing—
To be actually happier than the gods:
Anyone who, sitting opposite you,
Can look at you over and over again,
And hear you gently laughing . . .

Love and Hate (Catullus: *Poems,* 85)

I hate her
And at the same time I love her.

Perhaps you won't understand me—
And indeed I don't know what to think myself—
But it's true.

I am tortured by her.

Horace is a somewhat later imitator of the Greek lyricists. His tone is more careful and controlled than that of Catullus; his love poems have more charm than bite. He is more convincing in his poems about the delights of life in the Italian countryside, and his main skill is in his ordered use of the Latin language and his ability to make a very few words say a very great deal. Unlike Catullus, Horace's origins were humble. He had been enrolled in Brutus's army at the battle of Pharsalus, and although he had run away during the fighting and returned to Rome, his loyalty remained firm to the new regime, which he praised in six "State Odes" dedicated to the emperor.

XVI.3 Portrait of the poet Horace at a party in the country. (Museum of Fine Arts, Boston)

Readings

Harvest Festival (Horace: *Odes,* iii. 18)

Faunus—lover of the nymphs who flee before you:

Please move gently over my land
    And my sunny estate;
Please, when you go, be kind to all my young things.

At the end of the season,
I will sacrifice a young goat to you.
And I'll make sure that the bowl
    That Venus loves
Is filled to the brim with wine.
And I'll have my ancient altar smoking with incense . . .

The farmer who has been digging the earth
    Till he hates it
Will be happy dancing on it now: one and—two and—three.

Dulce et decorum est pro patria mori (Horace: *Odes*, iii. 2)

It is a fine and fitting end—to die for your country:
    But in any case, death follows you, even if you run away.
A young man who hates to fight will not be spared
    Just because his knees are knocking
    Or his frightened back is turned.

The third lyricist is Ovid: most of his life was uneventful but he
lived well on his income from his writing, which mingled passion,
irony, and dry humor with an engaging skill in telling a good story. He
was best known—and still is—for the *Metamorphoses*, a long poem
retelling all the Greek myths which involve someone being changed
into someone or something else, and finishing with the expectation
that Augustus will be changed into a god. At the same time, Ovid
wrote another popular work, the *Ars Amatoria*, a light-hearted instruc-
tion manual on seduction as well as a satire on the seamy side of
aristocratic life in Rome. Ovid clearly had first-hand knowledge here,
for he himself became entangled in a scandal (possibly with the emperor's daughter Julia), and Augustus deported him to Tomi, on the
shore of the Black Sea. Ovid's last book of poems, *Tristia*, was written
in exile, and it was an unsuccessful plea to be allowed to return to
Rome.

Reading

A Rough Voyage to Tomi (Ovid: *Tristia* i)

Gods of the sea and sky—what is left now except prayer?—
    Please don't shake apart the timbers of my poor ship.
Help! How huge are the mountains of water rearing up over us!
    You'd think they were about to touch the stars of heaven.
How deep are the valleys carved out by the water receding!
    You'd think they were about to touch the depths of hell.
Wherever I look—nothing but sea and sky:
    The one swollen with waves, the other angry with clouds.

And between them the gale, howling frightfully.
   The seas don't know which master to obey.
At the helm, the sailor hesitates: should he head into the wind,
      Or turn away? Among such horrors his seamanship is useless.

Epic Poetry: Vergil

Born in 70 B.C., as a young man Vergil went to Rome, where he came under the influence of the friends of Catallus. He gave up any idea of a life in politics when civil war broke out in 49 B.C. After Caesar's death, Vergil had supported Mark Antony, but Maecenas took him in hand and persuaded him (as well as Horace) to switch his allegiance to the new emperor.

Early in his career Vergil wrote the *Eclogues,* poems of country life in the style of the Greek writer Theocritus. Then came the *Georgics,* modeled on Hesiod's *Works and Days,* a didactic poem about farming that includes the most detailed surviving version of the story of Orpheus and Eurydice. Vergil's major work was an epic poem in twelve books in the style and meter of Homer called the *Aeneid* (the story of Aeneas). This poem was commissioned by Augustus in 26 B.C., and was nearly finished at Vergil's death in 19 B.C. On his deathbed, Vergil asked that the manuscript be destroyed, but Augustus pretended not to have received the message.

In the *Iliad,* it had been foretold that the descendants of Aeneas would one day rule over the Trojans. Moreover, stories of Aeneas's travels after his escape following the sack of Troy were familiar to the Romans in various versions. But after the wars in Macedonia ended, interest and admiration of Greek culture increased, and Romans now were stirred by the question: Why should Aeneas not have finished his journey in Italy? Why could he not then have become a forbear of the founders of the city? Thus the legends of early Rome could be happily linked with Greek tradition, while the Romans' patriotism could be satisfied by having the hero of the story not a Greek, but an enemy of the Greeks. Vergil skillfully adapted these somewhat tortuous sets of connections and gave them their final form in his epic. However, the narrative in the *Aeneid* is only the framework Vergil uses to set forth a detailed justification of Rome's manifest destiny to rule the world, along with passages in praise of the Roman character, of selected Roman historical heroes, and of the Italian landscape.

The format of the first half of the *Aeneid* closely follows that of the *Odyssey:* many of Aeneas's adventures are told in the first person to a listener who has rescued him from a shipwreck. Incidents in the *Odyssey*'s plot are echoed as well. For example, Aeneas meets the Cyclopes, is tempted by a seductress (Dido), and visits the underworld. The *Iliad* is the model for the second half of the *Aeneid.* In it are accounts of single combats, of funeral games, and of a new shield

Vulcan makes for Aeneas on which is depicted the Battle of Actium. Above all, however, Vergil never forgets that all human life and achievement is steeped in sadness: *Sunt lacrimae rerum* (Everywhere there are tears).

Readings

Aeneas Escapes from Troy (Vergil: *Aeneid*, ii. 720)

Over my head and shoulders I spread a lion skin, and settled my father on my back. My little son Ascanius took my right hand and stumbled after me. My wife Creusa came on behind. We walked through the darkness, and I, who had never been scared when I saw the Greek line of battle or when I was under fire from Greek javelins, now jumped at every movement; and every sound made me fear for my father and my son.

I was near the gates and seemed to have made my way to safety, when suddenly I heard the sound of marching feet. My father, looking out into the murk, called out: "Run, my boy, run; they're coming. I can see the flashing of their armor, the glitter of their shields."

And at that moment some evil spirit made me stop thinking what I was doing; I stepped off the path that I knew well, and found myself in a part of the city that I did not know. And where was Creusa? Vanished. She had missed the way or stopped for a rest, perhaps. I never saw her again . . .

I strapped on my armor and made my way back into the city; I was ready to take any risk, to face any danger, to go through the whole city if necessary. I explored along the walls, in the dark doorways which I had left earlier. I retraced every step, I searched everywhere . . .

I called Creusa's name again and again. And as I rushed on through the town, she appeared—or her shape did, unusually tall. I stood still, my hair on end and my voice sticking in my throat. Then she spoke to me in my misery: "What good does it do you to grieve me so madly? These things are the will of the gods—Jupiter has said that you may not take me away with you. A long exile is ahead of you, and a long voyage; but you will come at last to a land in the West, where the river Tiber flows gently through a fertile land. There you will find a happy future, and a kingdom—and a new wife, the daughter of a king."

Aeneas Visits the Underworld (Vergil: *Aeneid*, vi. 124, 236, 299)

The way down to Hell is easy: the black gate is open night and day. But to retrace your steps and to make your way into the upper air again—that is where the hard work lies. Only a few have ever been able to do it—those who were descended from the gods, or who were beloved of Jupiter and whose good deeds still shine brightly. . . .

There is a deep cave with a yawning, sharp-edged gap for its entrance, by a dark lake which is overshadowed by trees. No birds can fly by it in safety, for a jet of foul air spurts out from its black jaws up to the curved heaven above. The place is called Avernus—in Greek *a-ornos*, which means "without birds". . . .

The fearful Charon stands guard over the river bank, ghastly in his reeking filth. His beard is tangled, and his eyes glow above the stained cloak which he hunches around his shoulders. One hand is on the sheet, the other on the steering-pole of his dirty brown boat; he is the ferryman of the dead. Already he is incredibly ancient, but still young and green by the standards of the immortal gods.

And a great crowd rushes up to him—grown men and women, heroes of great reputation, along with boys and girls who have been placed on their funeral pyres before the eyes of their parents. They stand as thick as the leaves that fall at the first frost of autumn, or as the birds that come massing in to shore from the open sea when the cold weather drives them across the water to the warmth of the land. They stand begging to be the first to be allowed to make the crossing; they stretch out their hands to show Charon how much they long to reach the farther shore.

Roman History: Livy

The Romans were fascinated by their own past and read legends and history enthusiastically. The most distinguished historian during Augustus's reign was Livy, who came to Rome from northern Italy early in the Principate, and whose scholarship soon caught the emperor's attention. Livy wrote a *History of Rome*—in a hundred and forty-two books—from its foundation to his own time. Of this history, there have survived only those sections that deal with Rome's early history up to the sack of the city by the Gauls in 390 B.C. and with the Second Punic War, along with summaries of parts of the rest by ancient commentators. Livy's history was conceived as a prose epic to stand alongside the *Aeneid.* Thus many of the characters in it are larger than life, and in many incidents Livy shifted the emphasis from the actual facts to more romantic illustrations of the courage and integrity of great Romans of the past. As a source, then, Livy's work may be faulted for its lack of historical accuracy and objectivity. Yet it is still read and praised for its portrayal of history as drama, the unfolding of great events that build to a triumphant climax.

Chapter Seventeen

PAX ROMANA

*U*nlike Alexander the Great's empire, which collapsed soon after his death in 323 B.C., the constitution that Augustus had designed to govern Rome and its empire outlasted him comfortably, despite the varied character and competency of his successors. Some of these emperors were bad, some mad, but some were administrators of exceptional ability, men of wisdom and generosity. These emperors were mindful of the welfare of their people, and more often than not they were tolerant of the different religious and cultural traditions that characterized an empire covering most of what they thought to be the world. When there was resistance or rebellion, it expressed opposition to individual emperors, never to the institution of the empire itself.

This is not, however, the stuff to inspire exciting historical narrative. Contemporary historians tended to make the most of small-scale military movements, trivial diplomatic incidents, and the many scandals within the emperors' immediate circle. In reality, the course of the next two hundred years of Roman history included few examples of new political directions or ideas. Even significant social movements below the surface, such as the rise of Christianity, went largely unheralded and perhaps unrecognized by the Romans themselves.

THE JULIO-CLAUDIAN EMPERORS, A.D. 14–68

Tiberius A.D. 14–37

Augustus died exhausted in A.D. 14 at the age of seventy-seven. The Senate at once voted that he should become a god. Then, as was its formal right and as he had instructed them to do, the members of the Senate appointed his stepson Tiberius to be the next emperor. Tiberius, despite his unhappiness at the way he had been selected as Augustus's heir, began his reign with a period of solid though unspectacular government. But he soon showed the arrogance that always had been typical of his father's family. He could never forget that he had become emperor against his will, and he could not hide the fact that the daily duties and ceremonies of his job bored and depressed him.

When he had been adopted as Augustus's son, Tiberius had been required to bypass his own son Drusus as his heir, and instead to adopt his nephew Germanicus (so called for his highly successful northern campaigns). Now, the more moody and aloof Tiberius grew, the more popular Germanicus became. However, Germanicus died in his camp in A.D. 19. Roman gossip said that he either had been poisoned or his death had been caused by witchcraft—and that the emperor was behind it. When he heard the gossip, Tiberius's jealousy of Germanicus soon turned to fear of Germanicus's friends. He began to imagine plots against himself. He encouraged informers who would report to him insults against the emperor they had overheard, or simply disrespectful jokes. He ordered treason trials and even executions.

By A.D. 26, Tiberius had had enough of Rome. At the suggestion of the praetorian prefect Sejanus, he withdrew to his villa on Capri, where he is supposed to have indulged in unlovely vices and endless self-pity. Sejanus, left in charge in Rome, soon became too powerful for his own good. He was selective about what he thought the emperor should be

Relationship of Augustus's second wife Livia to the Julio-Claudian emperors

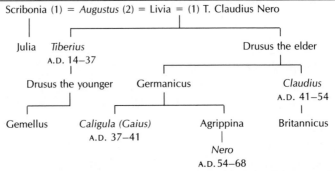

told, he appointed his own friends to army commands, and he began to ingratiate himself with the Senate and with Tiberius, in the hopes of being appointed the next emperor. But he lost the emperor's support when he was accused of having poisoned Tiberius's young son Drusus in order to clear his own path to power, and Tiberius had him tried by the Senate as a traitor, and put to death.

Another seemingly less important incident that occurred when Tiberius was in Capri was a disturbance in the province of Judaea, caused by that same Jesus who had been born in the stable during Augustus's census. For some years Jesus had been an itinerant religious teacher, finding most of his support among the poor people of the countryside. Calling himself the King of the Jews or the Son of God, he preached to anyone who would listen of the approaching establishment of God's kingdom. Jesus made as many enemies as friends, however, and the authorities became convinced that Jesus planned to lead a revolution against the Romans and to restore the deposed royal family of Judaea. Finally, infuriated by the mock-regal style of Jesus's arrival in Jerusalem in the spring of A.D. 33, a local magistrate named Pontius Pilate had him tried and crucified—the standard punishment for a non-Roman or slave found guilty of sedition. In Rome the affair was dismissed as just another incident in the unrest that was becoming common in Judaea.

Tiberius spent the last eleven years of his reign as a hermit on Capri, *solus et senex* (alone and old), and he died there in A.D. 37. However, he could not make up his mind whom he should commend to the Senate as his successor. Instead, he left it to the Senate to make the choice between Germanicus's son Gaius (nicknamed Caligula for the little army boots—*caligae*—he had worn as a child) and his own grandson, Gemellus. The Senate chose Caligula.

Readings

The Decline of the Senate (Tacitus: *Annals*, iii.65)

I have decided not to mention proposals made in the Senate unless they were remarkable for their clearsightedness, or they were the cause of a scandal. I think the purpose of history is to promise to record good deeds so that they can be praised, and to threaten to hold up bad words and actions for the disapproval of posterity.

But these times were so rife with depravity or ill-intentioned flattery that the leaders of the state had to protect their reputation by currying favor with others; those who had

already been consul, along with those who were yet to take up
public office, and a great many senators of no importance what-
soever, vied with each other in making inappropriate and toady-
ing proposals. They say that Tiberius, whenever he left the
Senate House, used to say: "They are fit to be nothing but
slaves." Even he, who saw no value in a free state, grew impatient with this general tolerance of servility.

The Purity of the Latin Language (Suetonius: *Lives of the Twelve Caesars*, Tiberius, 71)

Tiberius was fluent in Greek, but he normally spoke Latin,
especially on official occasions. He once apologized to the Senate because he had used the Greek word *monopoly*, because
there was no sufficiently exact word for this in Latin. He objec-
ted to the wording of a decree of the Senate because of the
inclusion of an obscure Greek term. "If you cannot find a Latin
equivalent," he ordered, "you must use a paraphrase." On another occasion, when a soldier of foreign birth was being questioned in a hearing, he ruled that the soldier must not answer
at all unless he could answer in Latin.

Jesus Avoids a Trick Question (*Gospel According to St. Luke*, 20 [King James version])

And the chief priests and the scribes . . . watched him, and
sent forth spies, which should feign themselves just men, that
they might take hold of his words, that so they might deliver
him into the power and authority of the governor.

And they asked him, saying, "Master, we know that thou
sayest and teachest rightly, neither acceptest thou the person of
any, but teachest the way of God truly: is it lawful for us to give
tribute unto Caesar, or no?"

But he perceived their craftiness, and said unto them,
"Why tempt ye me? Show me a penny. Whose image and super-
scription hath it?"

And they answered and said, "Caesar's."

And he said unto them, "Render therefore unto Caesar
the things which be Caesar's, and unto God the things which
be God's."

Caligula A.D. 37–41

The young Caligula, like his predecessor, started his reign well, but he soon fell ill and, on his recovery, seemed to have gone mad. He was rude to members of the Senate. He spent public money lavishly on his private entertainment. He took delight in being unexpectedly cruel to friends or even to total strangers, and he executed without trial those whom he imagined to be his enemies. He was even rumored by his critics to have made his horse a consul, and to have given it a marble stall and a purple blanket. As unrest grew in Rome, the praetorian guard decided to act. A few guards who could no longer tolerate his vices and excesses beat him to death in a corridor of his palace.

Reading

The Emperor's Disappointment (Suetonius: *Lives of the Twelve Caesars*, Caligula 30)

Caligula's favorite method of execution was to inflict upon his prisoner a series of small wounds which did not affect his vital organs. His order "Make this man aware that he is dying" was often quoted.

His favorite line of poetry was *Oderint dum metuant* (Let them hate me so long as they fear me).

He went about complaining that times were bad, particularly since there had been no famous disasters. "No one will remember my reign," he said, "because everyone is so well off." He often prayed for a military defeat, or for pestilence, fire, or famine—or failing all else an earthquake.

Claudius A.D. 41–54

Caligula had made no provision for a successor; but the praetorian guardsmen found his uncle, Claudius, hiding behind a curtain during all the confusion of the assassination. They dragged him out and proclaimed him emperor at once. The Senate had no stomach to disagree, though Claudius was indeed an unimpressive figure. He stammered, his face twitched, he limped; he seemed almost half-witted. Yet behind his physical deformities (perhaps caused by an attack of polio as a child) he had a keen mind; he had been a pupil of Livy and had written a book on Etruscan antiquities.

Claudius made no attempt to disguise his awkwardness, for he quickly realized that if his enemies did not take him seriously, they might relax their guard—and that would be all to the good. As it turned out, Claudius was a competent and imaginative administrator. He enlisted freedmen (ex-slaves) into the civil service and gave them significant responsibilities in his administration and in Rome's financial affairs. He granted Roman citizenship to provincials on a generous scale, and he seated a group of Gallic tribal chiefs in the Senate, to which he returned some of its decision-making powers.

Claudius' foreign policy was less conservative than that of Augustus or Tiberius. When Claudius was dissatisfied with the performance of three of the Eastern client-kings, he took away their kingdoms and turned them into provinces. A fourth province, Britain, was annexed apparently only because Claudius wanted to demonstrate that he was as capable of soldierly acumen as his brother Germanicus. He maintained order in Britain with an impressive show of force; the number of British place-names ending in "-chester" or "-cester" (*castra:* camp) indicates the size and spread of the Roman military presence there.

To celebrate the conquest of Britain Claudius nicknamed his son Britannicus. However, the boy was not to become his heir. Claudius's second wife Agrippina—she was the sister of Caligula, and thus also Claudius's niece—began to push the claims of her son by a previous marriage, Nero. Agrippina was a woman of ferocious determination, and Claudius was quite unable to stand up to her. In A.D. 54, Claudius died suddenly after eating a dinner of mushrooms that she was rumored to have poisoned. As a mark of its satisfaction at his reign, the Senate voted that Claudius, like Augustus, should become a god. But in deference to Agrippina it also voted that Nero was to become the new emperor.

Reading

A Freedman Abroad on Imperial Business (Tacitus: *Annals,* xiv.39)

Polyclitus, a slave who had obtained his freedom, was now sent to give a report on the situation in Britain. The emperor hoped that he would be able to exert enough authority to settle the quarrel between the governor and his deputy, and also to arrange peace among the restless natives. Polyclitus made his influence felt as he passed through Italy and Gaul with his entourage; then he crossed the Channel and instilled terror into the Roman troops there. But to the enemy he was a laughing stock, because they took their freedom seriously, and did not understand how so much power could be given to a freedman; they simply could not believe that a general, and an army which had just brought to an end such a significant campaign, could be obedient to a slave.

Nero A.D. 54–68

Like his predecessors, Nero made an excellent first impression, but the pathological insecurity of the Claudian family quickly asserted itself. Nero early began to resent his mother's constant presence. Agrippina appeared beside him at state functions, and had her portrait placed beside his on coins; on occasion she even slept with him. Finally, he decided to be rid of her and his young rival, Claudius's son Britannicus. Britannicus was poisoned and secretly buried; but Agrippina presented a more difficult problem, for she kept an armed guard always with her. On his first attempt Nero arranged a moonlit sail for Agrippina in a boat designed to fall apart when out at sea. The boat collapsed according to plan, but Agrippina was tougher than he expected, and she managed to swim ashore. The next time Nero took no chances. He simply hired a gang of thugs who broke into her villa and stabbed her to death.

Under Nero, the government of the empire continued to operate efficiently. For the most part, the provinces remained content and his financial and economic management was effective. He made life easier for merchants by dredging the harbor at Ostia, and he attempted to cut a canal through the isthmus of Corinth; at the groundbreaking ceremonies he dug the first spadeful in person, but the enterprise soon fell through. In any case, administration and public works soon took second place in Nero's mind to art and music. He had long fancied himself as a lyre-player and a composer, and he now became entirely preoccupied with private practice and public performance. He made tours of Italy, Greece, and Asia, entering competitions wherever he went—and winning all of them. Everywhere he was met by enthusiastic and sometimes genuine applause.

Music seemed a harmless hobby, and in the beginning it kept the emperor out of trouble; in the end, however, it made him forget reality altogether. In A.D. 64 a very serious fire destroyed much of the city of Rome; but apparently all that Nero did about it was to stand on the roof of his palace watching the blaze and reciting passages from the *Odyssey* about the sack of Troy. And there is no doubt that his behavior after the fire was equally callous. He showed little sympathy for the people who had lost their homes. Although he announced an extensive plan to rebuild the city, it turned out to be first and foremost a plan to construct ever more luxurious quarters for himself.

Nero had suddenly become unpopular, and unpopularity made him nervous. He therefore tried to distract attention from himself by bringing charges of arson against unspecified members of a new Jewish religious movement that recently had spread to Rome. The movement was named after its founder, Jesus, also known as Christ (derived from the Greek word for *"anointed"*). But Nero's attack on the Christians was purely a diversionary tactic. It had nothing to do with their beliefs, for Romans had always been tolerant of different religious systems. Throughout their history they had cheerfully mixed other peoples' religious ideas with their own, and particularly since the time of Augustus, Roman soldiers had brought back all sorts of exotic cults from Asia.

Their constant references to the coming of the Kingdom of God made it easy to accuse the Christians of crimes against the state. Furthermore, they had gone so far as to include women and slaves as equals in their community. By all reports they were cannibals as well. Did not their main ritual consist of eating the body of their founder? Their activities in Rome were supposed to be secret, and in fact they often hid themselves in underground caves. However, Nero hunted them down and sent them in large numbers into the circus to feed the lions, or to be tortured and then put to death. Legend says that among the early victims were Paul, who had first brought Jesus's teaching to Rome, and Jesus's disciple Peter, whose cathedral much later was to be built on the spot where Nero was supposed to have had him crucified.

Though ordinary Romans soon began to forget their frustration with Nero, some senators vigorously opposed his life of increasing extravagance and his obsession with his lyre. Rumors of plots against him began to circulate. Once more informers appeared, as they had against Tiberius, to spread the rumors, and Nero became ever more unbalanced. Disturbances broke out in Britain and in Judaea; there were mutinies among Roman troops in Gaul and on the German borders. The praetorian guard began to look to other candidates for emperor, and the Senate, regaining some of its old republican confidence, finally voted to depose Nero. In a fit of depression, Nero committed suicide. His last words were *"Qualis artifex pereo"* (What an artist the world will lose in me).

Readings

Rebellious Druids in Britain (Tacitus: Annals, xiv.29)

Suetonius Paulinus [the governor of Britain under Nero] next planned an attack on the island of Mona [Anglesey, off the coast of North Wales], which had a large population and also served as a sanctuary for refugees. The crossing was short but dangerous: the infantry were carried across in flat-bottomed boats, and a ford was found for the cavalry. The riders swam alongside their horses in the deeper parts.

On the opposite shore waited a mass of armed men and women standing shoulder to shoulder; the women were dressed in funeral robes, with their hair flying wild and torches in their hands, like the Furies. And the Druids, shouting out their prayers and shaking their fists, looked so strange that the Roman soldiers stood stock still, unable to defend themselves. But Suetonius barked at his troops, and they roused themselves not to be scared of a crowd of fanatics; they brought up their standards and pressed forward, contriving to set the British alight with their own firebrands. After the battle, the Romans established a garrison on the island and cut down the sacred groves where the British had been accustomed to perform their horrible rites: for many years the altars had run with the blood of prisoners and the intentions of the gods had been read in the entrails of human beings.

Boadicea, the Rebel Queen (Tacitus: Annals, xiv.34)

Suetonius drew up his infantry with a screen of archers, with the cavalry massed on the wings. But the British troops were everywhere at once, in small groups but in unprecedented numbers, so confident of victory that they had brought along their wives as spectators; the women were standing on farm-carts all around the battlefield.

Queen Boadicea had her daughters up with her in her chariot, and drove along the lines of the assembled British tribes, reminding them that the British were used to having a woman lead them into battle, and that she herself was descended from famous ancestors.

"But today," she said, "I am not defending my kingdom or my possessions; today I am an ordinary woman seeking vengeance.

"The Romans have taken away my freedom. The Romans have beaten me. The Romans have raped my daughters. Their greed has left no one untouched, not even the very old or the very young. But our gods will help us; they have already annihilated the one Roman legion which has dared to face us. The rest of them have been holed up in their camps, looking for a way of escape. There are thousands of us, and they are scared of our war-cries and our war-dances even before they have faced us in the field.

"Be ready to win this battle or to die. I am a woman, and that at least is what I shall do. If any man wants to stay alive, let him—it will only be in order to become a slave."

"THE YEAR OF THE FOUR EMPERORS,"
A.D. 68–69

With Nero gone, the Julio-Claudian line became extinct. The Senate appointed as the new emperor Galba, the governor of Spain. Then within a year (A.D. 68–69) Galba was followed onto the throne by three other emperors (all provincial governors), Otho, Vitellius, and Vespasian—each disputing the succession and each using his army to support his claim. It was a bewildering year at best; at worst, a dangerous one for politicians and generals. Many expected a return to the bad old days of the failing republic, and it was feared that the unusual number of fierce thunderstorms and lightning strikes that year only went to prove that the gods were more interested in punishing Rome than in preserving peace. But the inner strength Augustus had built into the machinery of his constitution held the empire together through the upheaval, and allowed it to survive into a steadier time.

THE FLAVIAN EMPERORS, A.D. 69–96

Vespasian (Flavius Vespasianus) the last of the "four emperors," reigned for ten years (A.D. 69–79). Vespasian was followed by his sons Titus (A.D. 79–81) and Domitian (A.D. 81–96). The Flavian emperors were dedicated to the restoration of stable government, and to improving the finances of the empire after Nero's irresponsible extravagance and the expenses of the wars of A.D. 68–69. To improve state finances, Vespasian introduced a group of new taxes. One of the most notable of these was the tax on urine, which was used to bleach togas (to this day in some parts of France a public urinal is known as "une Vespasienne.") More and more non-Italians were added as members of the Senate, so that it now became truly representative of the empire as a whole. Provincial administration, too, seemed to improve and become more efficient.

Remarkably few events of note occurred under the Flavian emperors. There were further conquests in Britain, and serious unrest in Judaea, which at last broke out into open revolt in A.D. 70. In Rome a triumphal arch and the amphitheatre known as the Colosseum were dedicated to commemorate the crushing of the Judean revolt by Titus. He sacked Jerusalem and destroyed the Temple, though the fortress of

The First Sixteen Roman Emperors, 27 B.C.–A.D. 180

The Julio-Claudian Emperors

Augustus	27 B.C.–A.D. 14
Tiberius	A.D. 14–37
(Caligula) Caius	A.D. 37–41
Claudius	A.D. 41–54
Nero	A.D. 54–68

The "Year of the Four Emperors"

Otho	A.D. 68–69
Galba	
Vitellius	
Vespasian	

The Flavians

Vespasian	A.D. 69–79
Titus	A.D. 79–81
Domitian	A.D. 81–96

The "Five Good Emperors"

Nerva	A.D. 96–98
Trajan	A.D. 98–117
Hadrian	A.D. 117–138
Antoninus Pius	A.D. 138–161
Marcus Aurelius	A.D. 161–180

Masada held out until A.D. 73, a battle against long odds that stands in history alongside the defense of Thermopylae. Augustus's tolerant policy toward the Jews was now reversed, and the persecution of the Christians, who now were not necessarily distinguished from the Jews, continued sporadically until the end of Domitian's reign.

At home there was a natural disaster. In A.D. 79 the volcano of Vesuvius, near Naples on the coast south of Rome, erupted, burying the seaside resorts of Pompeii and Herculaneum under a deep layer of lava and ash. Apparently, there was enough warning for most of the inhabitants to escape. But the houses and shops were hurriedly abandoned and they were preserved by the lava and ash with many of their artifacts nearly intact: furniture, pots and pans, lamps, frescoes, mosaics, jewelry—even food in cupboards, meals on tables, and the graffiti on the walls. Although the two towns remained buried for the next seventeen hundred years, their excavation provided a complete record of ordinary daily life in an ordinary, fairly prosperous Roman town of the early empire. One of the few victims was the famous naturalist Pliny the Elder, who lingered too long in order to find out what a volcanic eruption looked like up close; an eyewitness account of the eruption has survived in a letter written by his nephew, Pliny the Younger.

The literature of the Flavian period is also worthy of attention. Historians now were freed from the necessity to flatter or appease the

XVII.1 The interior of the Colosseum: raked rows of seats and multiple entrances at different levels resemble the layout of a modern stadium. The floor of the arena (now lost) was covered with sand to soak up any spilled blood; and below the arena were the dressing rooms and cages for the animals. (Photograph by Peter Clayton)

emperors, as well as from some of the more formal literary conventions typical of the Augustan style. Suetonius' short biographies in the *Lives of the Twelve Caesars* (from Julius Caesar to Domitian) are sprinkled with gossip incapable of proof. Even though they would certainly today not be admissible as history or even journalism, they remain exceedingly entertaining. Suetonius's contemporary, Tacitus, is great deal more somber, and openly hostile to Tiberius and Nero; but he is certainly worth reading for his ingenious epigrammatic style. Tacitus's *Annals* are a history of Rome in the time of the Julio-Claudian emperors (with the accounts of Caligula and most of Claudius lost). His *Histories* deal with the year of the four emperors. He also wrote a study of the German tribes, which is full of interesting information about the peoples who would later overrun the empire, and a biography of his father-in-law Agricola, governor of Britain.

Also written in this same period were the *Satires* of Juvenal, poems lampooning the habits and eccentricities of urban Romans, and the *Institutes* of Gaius, an account of the principles of Roman law. The title sounds dull, but they are lucidly written and are still consulted by law students.

The Flavian dynasty ended with the assassination of Domitian in A.D. 96. Like Tiberius, Domitian had become obsessed with treason and plots against his life and had turned cruel and capricious. After his death, his statues were pulled down and all inscriptions bearing his name were chipped out. Even so, it was a sign of the general stability in Roman affairs that the Senate was able to choose his successor without any pressure from the army, and for the first time from among one of their own members: an elderly lawyer named Nerva.

Reading

Vesuvius and Pompeii (Pliny the Younger: *Letters,* vi)

About the seventh hour [1:00 P.M.], my mother noticed a cloud of unusual size and shape. She called for her sandals and went up to a higher place where she could better observe the strange sight. A cloud was rising up from a mountaintop—later on we realized it was Mount Vesuvius—which resembled a pinetree more than anything else; it rose up in a long column like a trunk, and then spread out sideways like branches. To my uncle [Pliny the Elder] it meant only a phenomenon which must be examined more closely: he ordered a boat to be got ready, and told me I could come with him if I wanted. I said I had some work to do—by chance he himself had just given me a topic to write up. As he left the house, he received a note from Rectina, who was very frightened: her house lay right below the mountain, and there was no way she could get out except by boat. She begged him to rescue her from this fearful danger. So my uncle made plans to take boats across, and himself embarked to bring help not only to Rectina but to many other people. . . .

Ash was by now falling on the boat, along with pieces of black pumice and red-hot stones. My uncle waited a little, then said to the helmsman: "Fortune favors the brave. Go to Pomponianus." Pomponianus was at Stabiae [five miles south of Pompeii]; he had loaded his possessions onto boats, sure he would have to take flight if the wind should change. My uncle arrived, embraced him and tried to cheer him up . . . but his courtyard was now filling up with ash and pumice, so that if he stayed in his house any longer, he would not be able to get out. My uncle approached Pomponianus and the others, and they consulted together. He decided to go down to the beach and see if he could get away from there: but the sea was running very high. So he spread out a sail for shelter—and constantly had cold water brought to him to drink.

The flames and stink of sulphur drove everyone else away, but they merely excited my uncle's curiosity. He was helped to his feet by a couple of slaves, but then collapsed. He could not breathe because of the thick smoke, and in any case he suffered from asthma. The next day, his body was found without a mark upon it; he looked as if he were asleep rather than dead.

When my uncle had left, I got on with the work that had kept me behind. Soon I went to the baths and had dinner; my sleep was restless and I woke up frequently. For several days previously there had been earthquakes—not particularly frightening because earthquakes are common in Campania. But the shocks got stronger during the night, and things seemed not so much to be shifting about but to be altogether turned upside down. My mother came into my room just at the moment when I was getting up to see if she was still asleep. We stayed in the courtyard, and I called for a book of Livy's history; I read and made notes just as if nothing unusual were happening. A friend of my uncle who had just got back from Spain then turned up; when he saw my mother and me sitting in the courtyard—and me actually reading —he was angry that we appeared to be, in our various ways, so unconcerned. But I concentrated on my book. It was now six o'clock in the morning. The house was shaking, and there seemed to be a real risk that it would collapse. It did now seem sensible to leave the house. A great many people followed us and hurried us on; they were really frightened.

Outside the town we stopped; there was much to wonder at, and much to be afraid of. Our wagons were rolling in all directions, though we were on completely flat ground, and would not stay still even though we blocked their wheels with stones. We saw an earthquake make the sea pull back from the beach, leaving the shore covered with sea-creatures high and dry on the sand. In the other direction the black cloud flickered with jets of flame, like lightning flashes but bigger. Then our friend from Spain said, more insistently than ever, "If your uncle is still alive, he will want you to go somewhere safe. If he's dead, he will want you to survive him. What are you waiting for?" Without waiting for an answer he rushed off and made his way as quickly as he could to safety.

Soon the cloud hung down even lower, and entirely covered the sea. The ash, which we had not noticed much so far, was now all over the place. I looked back. Behind us was a thick pall of smoke; and it was dark—not the dark of a moonless cloudy night, but the dark of a closed room with the lights out. You could hear women crying, babies whimpering, men shouting; some were calling for their parents, some for their children, some for their spouses. Some were lamenting their own fate, some that of their nearest and dearest. Some in their fear of death prayed for death; many people lifted up their hands to the gods, but a greater number suggested that there were no gods anymore and that the world was drowning in perpetual night. At last the darkness faded away till it looked like smoke or a cloud; soon it was full daylight, and the sun shone again. We went back to Misenum where, unharmed in ourselves, we spent an anxious night balanced between hope and fear.

THE "FIVE GOOD EMPERORS," A.D. 96–180

The next group of Roman emperors were not members of the same family or related to each other in any way, but each had the good sense to choose a successor early in his reign, to adopt him into his family according to precedent, and to train him carefully to ensure a smooth transition of power.

This system allowed almost a century of uninterrupted stability and order, during which the emperors and the Senate worked together

ROMAN EMPIRE AT ITS GREATEST EXTENT 138 AD

in cooperative harmony. More and more people in the provinces became citizens—until the process became automatic in A.D. 212. Private philanthropy became a general custom: libraries, schools, and universities were founded by individual benefactors throughout the provinces and then partly funded by the state.

Many of the great surviving monuments of Roman architecture date from this century: aqueducts in Spain and Gaul, the temple of Zeus Olympios in Athens, Hadrian's defensive wall built across the width of Britain. In Rome itself are Hadrian's villa, the new and improved *insulae* at Ostia, and the Pantheon, the domed temple built by Trajan but fronted by an earlier porch dedicated by Augustus's colleague Agrippa.

Literature of this period was characterized by a revival of historical writing in Greek: Arrian produced his account of Alexander the Great's conquests, Josephus his *History of the Jewish War* (the revolt of A.D. 70), and Plutarch wrote his *Parallel Lives* (paired biographies of distinguished Greeks and Romans).

XVII.2 Portrait bust of a Roman citizen of African origin. (Museum of Fine Arts, Boston)

Nerva reigned only two years (A.D. 96–98), and was followed by Trajan (A.D. 98–117), who had the distinction of being the first emperor born outside Italy: he was born in Spain and had a Spanish mother. On a celebratory column, that still stands in Rome, is carved in relief a series of scenes commemorating Trajan's conquest of Dacia (modern Romania), the last province to be added to the Roman empire. Hadrian (A.D. 117–138) followed Trajan as emperor, and it was under him that the Roman empire reached its widest extent, covering most of Western and Southern Europe, Asia Minor, the Middle East and North Africa— an area roughly equal in size to the United States east of the Rockies. Most of Hadrian's time was spent on tours of inspection in the provinces. The inhabitants were grateful for his attention and he became popular and respected. The exception to the general stability and prosperity in the empire was Judaea; after a second revolt there in A.D. 135, the name of the province was changed to Syria Palestina. Jerusalem was rebuilt, as a city which no Jews were allowed to enter, and their exclusion led to the break-up of the important Christian community in the city. However, the official policy against the Christians was softened by both Trajan and Hadrian, who sent letters to provincial magistrates instructing that Christians were to be left strictly alone as long as they were not involved in political agitation.

XVII.3 Portrait of a young man from the province of Egypt. (Museum of Fine Arts, Boston)

The reigns of the next two emperors marked the triumph of the *Pax Romana*. The eighteenth-century English historian Edward Gibbon wrote of Hadrian's successor, Antoninus Pius (A.D. 138–161), that he "diffused order and tranquillity over the greatest part of the earth. His reign is marked by the rare advantage of furnishing very few materials for the historian." The next emperor, Marcus Aurelius (A.D. 161–180), personified the virtue and wisdom of Stoic philosophy. Marcus Aurelius is the only emperor who became as famous for his ethical teaching—recorded in his *Meditations*—as for his policies. If Plato had been alive, might he have seen in Marcus Aurelius the nearest approach that a mortal has made to the ideal of the philosopher-king?

Chapter Eighteen

DECLINE AND FALL

A cliff may look as if it will stand forever; yet centuries of surf beating upon it will slowly erode it piece by piece, at a rate invisible to the naked eye. No one alive in the first few decades that followed the reigns of "the five good emperors" could have known that the empire was beginning the long slide toward its end. With hindsight, however, the signs of Rome's decline were already clearly visible. Historians do not know for certain the causes of the Roman empire's collapse. But most of them are agreed that it fell because of a complex combination of moral, political, economic, and military failures, rather than any single phenomenon, such as (as one suggestion goes) the slow poisoning of most of the population by lead in the waterpipes.

The first omen of future problems became evident in the reign of Marcus Aurelius. The excellence of Marcus Aurelius's character was not matched by his wife's. Her influence, rather than his, was to be seen in their dissolute and worthless son, Commodus, who nevertheless was raised to become the next emperor. Under Commodus and his successors, Rome entered a period of intermittent chaos, in which the Senate once more dithered feebly while the army, especially the praetorian guard, selected its own emperors. On one occasion the empire was put up for auction to the highest bidder; and on another it was awarded to a soldier as a prize in a wrestling competition. These later emperors turned into despots who stripped the Senate of its last scraps of authority. They surrounded themselves more and more with luxurious accommodations and customs copied from the kingdoms of the East; and they abandoned the title of *Princeps,* and replaced it with *Dominus* (Lord and Master).

With their own extravagance everywhere unconfined, the emperors became unable to balance their budgets. The expenses of public services and public works, along with the salaries of the bureaucrats who directed them, ran out of control, and the economy began to fail. For generations the large numbers of available slaves had made agriculture and construction cheap, and there had been no need for technological innovation to make the work more efficient. (A contractor had once come to Vespasian with an idea for a crane to lift columns of a new temple into position; the emperor had paid the man for his idea, and then had refused to use it—in part, no doubt, to ensure that slaves did not become redundant and therefore restless or even dangerous.) But now that foreign conquests were a thing of the past, the supply of slaves at last began to dry up. And the Romans, who always distrusted change in any case, found themselves with few ideas of how to replace their labor.

In any case, farmland everywhere was becoming exhausted. As the fertility of the soil wore out, farms were abandoned and the land

XVIII.1 A battle between Romans and barbarians on the northern borders of the empire. (Bettmann Archive)

reverted to wilderness. Similarly, many mines now were worked out, and raw materials were becoming scarce. A drop in production of all kinds led to a decrease in population throughout the empire, which in turn began to adversely affect the state's income from taxes, as well as the number of recruits available for the armies stationed along the empire's frontiers. In any case, over the years Rome's soldiers had been replaced by a new generation of men from the provinces who largely lacked traditional Roman discipline and military dedication. Were pressure to be applied along the frontiers of the empire by barbarian tribes, the new Roman army would find it impossible to defend them.

And so it happened. The first border raids by the barbarians came as early as A.D. 256, followed by a respite for the next hundred and fifty years. During this period, the Roman empire was divided in two, for administrative and military convenience. In A.D. 330, the emperor Constantine moved the capital of the empire from Rome to Byzantium, which he renamed Constantinople. By this time he also had become the first emperor to convert to Christianity. In a ruling issued in A.D. 312, known as the Edict of Milan, Constantine granted Christians full freedom to worship as they wished, and instituted Sunday as a day off from work for everyone. Constantine also presided over the Council of Nicaea, which emerged the wording of the Nicene Creed, a formal statement of the dogma of the Catholic Church. Christianity became the official religion of the empire. Its two centers were Rome and Constantinople, with recognition of the seniority of the bishop of Rome.

XVIII.2 Mosaic from the province of Africa. A donkey (the favorite animal of Vesta, goddess of the hearth) nurses two lion cubs, in a parody of the tradition about the upbringing of Romulus and Remus. (Museum of Fine Arts, Boston)

In A.D. 364 the empire was finally and formally split into eastern and western halves, each with its own emperor. The eastern half settled down into long centuries of prosperity. Eventually known as the Byzantine Empire, with Constantinople as its capital, it lasted until the fifteenth century A.D. The western half, however, came under fierce attack from barbarian tribes. From Germany, the Vandals swarmed into Gaul, Spain, and Africa. Alaric the Goth invaded Italy and in A.D. 410 temporarily occupied Rome. Britain was evacuated as a result of uprisings by the Scots and the Saxons. Attila the Hun, in turn, ravaged Gaul and Italy. In A.D. 455, Rome was destroyed by the Vandals and left in ruins; and twenty years later, in A.D. 476, the last Roman emperor was deposed. There was no last gallant defiance, no final resistance, no drumrolls. The world at large took little notice of Rome's fall. The only thing memorable about the last of the Caesars is his name, which by a final irony was Romulus Augustulus.

Chapter Nineteen

EXEGI MONUMENTUM AERE PERENNIUS . . .

(I have built a monument to last longer than bronze—Horace)

*I*f history were fiction, the story of the Roman empire would have ended with the reign of Marcus Aurelius. After his rule, everything moved toward a sad anticlimax, a dying fall that goes on for much too long. It is preferable, in fact, to remember Rome as it was in A.D. 180— a powerful empire at its height, whose citizens, even though they comprised many different cultures, traditions, and religious beliefs, were apparently as content and unharried as any subject peoples have ever been. To be fair, however, we must remember that we have very little evidence about what these subject peoples may have thought about their situation. Ancient history in general says little about anyone except the rich and famous.

But history is not fiction, and it must consider and analyze with equal seriousness the worst as well as the best of times in any civilization. As history should, Roman history provides lessons and warnings that we may regard with both pity and terror, as well as living memories and a remarkable heritage that we should recognize with gratitude.

CONSTITUTION AND LAW

Many modern constitutions have borrowed ideas from the Roman republic—in particular its essential principle of governmental checks and balances. And these constitutions also often have suffered from its

137

XIX.1 Eighteenth century etching by Piranesi: "View of the Cow Field." This unromantic name was given to the abandoned Forum in the Middle Ages, and it stuck until the Renaissance. The Corinthian columns on the right belong to the temple of Castor and Pollux; the frontispiece shows the same columns from the opposite point of view. In the background, left center, is the Colosseum. (Museum of Fine Arts, Boston)

flaws. What is certain is that Roman law, as codified by Gaius under the Flavian emperors, is today the basis of all European legal systems (except English Common Law) and of the laws of the United States.

More importantly, Roman history shows a constitution can work only when it is doing the job for which it was originally designed, and demonstrates how it can fall apart when it fails to adapt to a changing political environment. Like the story of fifth century B.C. Athens, Roman history, too, illustrates how a democracy can fail when the people become jealous of their privileges but careless of their responsibilities, when the government's decisions reflect the shifting will of an unthinking majority rather than what is truly right and just.

LANGUAGE

Roman soldiers brought Rome with them wherever they served, and in the Western provinces their presence was so pervasive that Latin tended to supplant the native languages. But in these various provinces, Latin changed over the years as it was mixed with elements of the local variants and dialects, and eventually became the "Romance" languages of western Europe: French, Portuguese, Romanian, Spanish, and of course Italian. Latin also became one of several important linguistic strands in English, and much of English vocabulary is derived from Latin. Today, Latin phrases are found on many official seals and are inscribed on public buildings. They serve as mottoes and insignia of political, military, and academic institutions—for example, *e pluribus unum, semper fidelis, lux et veritas*. Furthermore, many Latin words and expressions have been borrowed unchanged in the terminology of law, literary criticism, and science, and even in daily conversation.

Until well into the twentieth century, Latin was the language of the Roman Catholic Church and of college and university ceremonials. Latin also was widely taught in secondary schools in Europe and the United States (and in a few civilized enclaves it still is). It also was routinely used in scholarly treatises until late in the eighteenth century. When a botanical essay written in English was submitted to a professor at Cambridge University about 1800, it was rejected because the professor "could not stomach the notion of degrading such a science by treating of it in a modern language." Of course, Latin is still used in taxonomy, where a new Latin formulation comes into existence whenever a new species is discovered. Roman numerals also are still used to mark clockfaces, calendars, and chapter headings in books, as well as to distinguish kings, queens, popes, children with the same names as their forebears, and American football championships. For computation, however, they were soon supplanted by the Arabic numerals that came by way of Constantinople.

LITERATURE

Even after Rome had disappeared, its literature was saved. Though filled with references to pagan gods and rituals, it was faithfully preserved by Christian monks in Europe and Muslim scholars in Byzantium. All through the Middle Ages, Roman manuscripts were copied, annotated, and studied, until they were once more published during the Renaissance. During the Renaissance, Latin and Greek works first began to be translated into English. North's version of Plutarch, for

SOME LATIN EXPRESSIONS IN EVERYDAY USE	
ad hoc/ad hominem	per se
alias/alibi	persona non grata
ante bellum	quid pro quo
e.g. (exempli gratia)	q.v. (quod vide)
et cetera	sine die
ibid. (ibidem)	sine qua non
i.e. (id est)	status quo ante
in loco parentis	sub par (paribus)
in statu pupillari	sub poena
inter alia	sui generis
ipso facto	v. (versus [in law] or vide)
mirabile dictu	vade mecum
nihil obstat, imprimatur	vice versa
op. cit. (opus citatum)	vs. (versus)

instance, appeared just in time for Shakespeare, who had "small Latin, and less Greek," to use it extensively as a source for his three "Roman plays" (*Coriolanus, Julius Caesar,* and *Antony and Cleopatra*).

Plots and themes from Roman history, legend, and mythology, as well as references to Latin literature, occur frequently throughout Western literature, and are one of its common denominators and pervasive influences. Until recently, most Western writers and speakers were familiar with Latin literature, and many of them had read the original works. It is not surprising, then, to find a Latinate influence in the style of many literary figures in Western culture.

THE TRANSMISSION OF GREEK CULTURE

Much of what has been said about the later influence of the Romans also involves the diffusion of the culture of the Greeks, who were, after all, a major influence on the Romans. From the third century B.C., it was the Romans who kept Greek ideas alive, after Greece itself had been absorbed into the empire. Romans removed Greek art and artifacts from Greece, and gathered them in their private collections, and had them reproduced in large quantities. They also adopted Greek styles in architecture, which with important Roman modifications later became a major influence in public and private buildings throughout Europe and America; for instance, the Cathedral in St. Petersburg, St. Paul's Cathedral in London, Thomas Jefferson's Monticello in Virginia, the Capitol in Washington, D.C., and ceremonial arches in Paris, London, and New York.

Some Latin Phrases Still Commonly Used

ars gratia artis: art for art's sake.

caveat emptor: let the buyer beware.

cave canem: beware of the dog.

carpe diem: seize the day (grab your opportunities while you can).

cogito, ergo sum: I think, therefore I am.

cui bono?: who benefits?

ex Africa semper aliquid novi: something new is always coming out of Africa.

eheu fugaces, Postume, Postume, labuntur anni: alas, Postumus, the years are slipping away.

gaudeamus igitur, iuvenes dum sumus: so let us be happy, while we are still young.

homo sum: nihil humanum alienum puto: I am a member of the human race—I believe that nothing that has to do with humanity is irrelevant to me.

Ignorantia legis neminem excusat: not to know the law is no excuse for anyone.

in medias res: straight to the heart of the matter.

mens sana in corpore sano: a healthy mind in a healthy body

parturiunt montes, nascitur ridiculus mus: the mountains are in labor, and a silly little mouse is born (you're making a mountain out of a molehill).

pro bono publico: for the public good.

quis custodiet ipsos custodes?: who will guard the guards themselves?

sic transit gloria mundi: worldly things last only briefly.

solitudinem faciunt, pacem appellant: they make a desert and they call it peace.

tempus fugit: time flies.

tot homines, quot sententiae: there are as many opinions as there are people to have them.

vivat rex/regina: long live the king/queen

The Romans brought Greek literature to Italy and made it the centerpiece of their own literary experience and of their educational syllabus. Greek manuscripts were collected and studied in Roman libraries, and they, too, were transferred safely to the medieval monasteries. Much of what the modern world knows of the Greeks, and much of what it owes to the Greeks, is a gift of the Romans.

CHRISTIANITY

It is hard to imagine that Christianity ever would have emerged as a world religion without the Romans. Christianity began in a Roman province, and from there spread throughout the Mediterranean world along Roman roads and in Roman ships. Its first missionary, Paul, was a Roman citizen, who traveled widely through much of the empire, preaching the gospel and writing letters. His experiences, recounted in the *Acts* and his various *Epistles* in the New Testament, were written in Greek so that they would be understood in the Eastern provinces.

The early church was organized on the model of the Roman empire—the Pope was emperor, his bishops were proconsuls, and their dioceses were provinces. As some of Christianity's original Jewish tenets were dropped, it gradually absorbed from Rome and Constantinople some of the ethical teachings of Plato and the Stoic philosophers. About A.D. 330, the Bible was published for the first time in an authorized Latin version (the *Vulgate*); the Old Testament was translated from the Hebrew and the New Testament from the Greek. The general acceptance of Christianity in the west was marked by the adoption of Latin as the language of church liturgy.

In the East, after Christianity became the accepted religion, the oracle at Delphi was closed in A.D. 391 by the emperor Theodosius. From Constantinople and its Cathedral of Saint Sophia emerged the Eastern Orthodox Church. In 1453 the Muslim capture of Constantinople compelled the church to reestablish itself in Greece and in Russia.

In Rome, the bishops and monks were more successful than the Roman emperors had been in withstanding the barbarian invasions. The Roman Catholic Church and its monasteries throughout Europe managed to survive and finally to flourish. The Church's proselytizing energy, for good or ill, then helped shape much of the subsequent history of the West—the warfare, politics, and diplomacy of the Middle Ages, the Renaissance and Reformation, and the Spanish Inquisition. Persecutions of Christians have led to wars, to migrations, and to discoveries of new worlds. Moreover, Christian missionaries have disseminated far more than scripture throughout the world. Church doctrine on the divine right of kings, the separation of church and state, arguments about heresy and papal infallibility, have affected the thinking and values of millions of people. Today, the Judeo-Christian and the Greco-Roman traditions are still entwined and remain powerful forces, standing their ground on the seven hills of the Eternal City.

SUGGESTED BIBLIOGRAPHY

PRIMARY SOURCES

Nearly all of the major primary sources for Roman civilization are quoted or mentioned in this book (see index). For more details on these and other sources, students should refer to the relevant entries in the *Cambridge Ancient History*, the *Oxford Classical Dictionary*, or the bibliographies of modern histories. The writers listed below wrote in Latin unless otherwise indicated; some translations are easier to find than others, but all can be found in the Loeb Library series (Harvard University Press) and many of them are included in the Penguin Classics series.

Early Roman History—to the Punic Wars

Livy: *History*
Plutarch (Greek): *Lives*

The Punic Wars to 133 B.C.

Cato: *On Agriculture*
Livy: *History*
Lucretius: *De Rerum Natura (The Nature of the Universe)*
Plautus: comedies
Plutarch (Greek): *Lives*
Terence: comedies

also Polybius (Greek, 2nd century B.C.): *Histories*

The Roman Revolution, 133–31 B.C.

Caesar: *Gallic War, Civil War*
Catullus: *Poems*
Cicero: political and forensic speeches, essays and letters
Plutarch (Greek): *Lives*
Suetonius: *Lives of the Twelve Caesars*

also Sallust (1st century B.C.): *War with Jugurtha, Catiline's Conspiracy*

The Principate of Augustus, 27 B.C.–14 A.D.

Augustus: *Res Gestae*
Horace: *Odes*
Ovid: *Metamorphoses*, etc.
Suetonius: *Lives of the Twelve Caesars*
Tacitus: *Annals*
Vergil: *Eclogues, Georgics, Aeneid*

also Vitruvius (early 1st century A.D.): *On Architecture*

The Julio-Claudian Emperors, A.D. 14–68

Bible, New Testament: *Gospels, Acts, Epistles*
Suetonius: *Lives of the Twelve Caesars*
Tacitus: *Annals*

The Later Emperors, A.D. 68–180

Marcus Aurelius: *Meditations*
Gaius: *Institutes*
Josephus (Aramaic, translated into Greek): *The Jewish War*
Juvenal: *Satires*
Pliny the Elder: *Natural History*
Pliny the Younger: *Letters*
Suetonius: *Lives of the Twelve Caesars*
Tacitus: *Histories, Agricola, Germania*

also Apicius (4th century A.D.): a collection of recipes
    Apuleius (2nd century A.D.): *The Golden Ass* (a novel)

SECONDARY SOURCES

There are many good modern histories, some easier and more accessible than others. A good place to look for more detailed treatments of particular topics is the *Cambridge Ancient History* (a twelve-volume treatment of all aspects of ancient civilization, in the form of a series of long articles by distinguished historians) and the *Oxford Classical Dictionary* (very clearly written entries on individuals and events as well as on cultural and social topics).

General Histories

John Boardman, J. Griffin, and O. Murray, eds., *Oxford History of the Classical World* (Oxford: Oxford University Press, 1986). A one-volume alternative to the *Cambridge Ancient History* by a newer generation of scholars.

M. Cary and H. H. Scullard, *A History of Rome*, 3d ed. (New York: St. Martins Press, 1976). For many years the standard basic history; very thorough and very staid.

Edward Gibbon, *The Decline and Fall of the Roman Empire*, 3 vols. (New York: Random House, 1977). (Also available in many other editions e.g., Encyclopaedia Britannica Great Books Series.) Written in the eighteenth century, but still famous for its command of detail as well as its elegant Latinate style.

Fritz M. Heichelheim, Cedric Yeo, and Allen M. Ward, *A History of the Roman People*, 2d ed. (Englewood Cliffs, NJ: Prentice-Hall, 1984). An up-to-date alternative to Cary and Scullard.

H. H. Scullard, *A History of the Roman World, 753 to 146 B.C.* (London: Routledge, 1991). *From the Gracchi to Nero*, 5th ed. (London: Routledge, 1982). Very thorough and easy to read.

Biographies/Special Topics

Michael Batterberry and Ariane Ruskin, *Greek and Roman Art* (New York: McGraw-Hill, 1968). Useful text, excellent colored illustrations.

Ernle Bradford, *Hannibal* (New York: Dorset Press, 1981). A straightforward account of Hannibal and the Second Punic War.

Roger Bruns, *Julius Caesar* (New York: Chelsea House, 1988). Includes useful information about Caesar's Rome as well as about Caesar himself. This and other biographies in Chelsea House's *World Leaders: Past and Present* series are specifically written for secondary school readers.

Moses I. Finley, *Aspects of Antiquity* (New York: Viking-Penguin, 1977). Very readable essays by a famous scholar.

Dorothy Hoobler and Thomas Hoobler, *Cleopatra* (New York: Chelsea House, 1987). Simply told but full of interesting detail.

Alexander Humez and Nicholas Humez, *ABC Et Cetera* (Boston: Godine, 1987). Amusing essays on various aspects of Roman life, based on the letters of the Roman alphabet.

Sarah Pomeroy, *Goddesses, Whores, Wives, and Slaves: Women in Classical Antiquity* (New York: Schocken, 1975). A clear, scholarly account of the position of women in Greek and Roman society.

David Stockton, *Cicero* (New York: Oxford University Press, 1988). A political biography of Cicero, detailed but not difficult to read.

Ronald Syme, *Roman Revolution* (Oxford: Oxford University Press, 1939). More than fifty years old, but still a seminal account of the fall of the Roman republic.

Nancy Z. Walworth: *Augustus Caesar* (New York: Chelsea House, 1989). A clear, straightforward outline of the first Roman emperor's life.

Novels
(nearly all titles are available in paperback)

Edward G. Bulwer-Lytton, *The Last Days of Pompeii* (New York: The Heritage Press, 1957). (Also available in many other editions.) Long and very Victorian in style, but still interesting as a forerunner of disaster books and films.

Robert Graves, *I, Claudius* (New York: Random House, 1977). Fictional autobiography of the emperor Claudius (also the basis of the PBS television series).

———, *Claudius the God.* The sequel to *I, Claudius.*

Peter Green: *The Sword of Pleasure* (London: John Murray, 1957). A fictional autobiography of Sulla.

Colleen McCullough, *The First Man in Rome: Marius* (New York: Morrow, 1990). Novel about the rivalry between Marius and Sulla.

Thornton Wilder, *The Ides of March* (New York: Harper, 1948). A fictional history of Caesar's dictatorship.

John E. Williams: *Augustus* (New York: Viking, 1972). A fictional biography of Augustus.

Plays

Albert Camus:	*Caligula*
Shakespeare:	*Coriolanus,*
	Julius Caesar
	Antony and Cleopatra
George Bernard Shaw:	*Androcles and the Lion*
	Caesar and Cleopatra

Films

A Funny Thing Happened on the Way to the Forum (musical comedy)

Androcles and the Lion (Maurice Evans, Jean Simmons—based on Shaw's play)

Ben Hur (famous for the chariot race scene)

Caesar and Cleopatra (Vivien Leigh, Claude Rains—based on Shaw's play)

Cleopatra (Elizabeth Taylor and Richard Burton)

Fellini's Satyricon (funny and decadent)

Julius Caesar (Marlon Brando, John Gielgud)

Quo Vadis? (a romance about the early Christians)

Seven Brides for Seven Brothers (musical comedy)

Spartacus (the Slave Revolt as high adventure)

The Life of Brian (Monty Python)

INDEX